LOCATION OF PUBLIC ENTERPRISES AND REGIONAL DEVELOPMENT

LOCATION OF PUBLIC ENTERPRISES AND REGIONAL DEVELOPMENT

AMITABH KUNDU
GIRISH K. MISRA
RAJKISHOR MEHER

CONCEPT PUBLISHING COMPANY, NEW DELHI

First Published 1986

Published by

Naurang Rai
Concept Publishing Company
H-13, Bali Nagar
NEW DELHI-110015 (India)

Printed in India by

Printway India
at S. Narayan and Sons
7117/18, Pahari Dhiraj,
DELHI-110006

To
Mirza Fahim Beg
who has seen Bhopal
live with the Heavy Electricals (India) Ltd.,
and die with the Union Carbide

PREFACE

THE process of industrialisation has a major role to play in the economic development of the underdeveloped states and regions in India. The disparity in the per capita income between the developed and the underdeveloped states is generally reflected in the structure of their economies—the former having a relatively developed industrial base while in the latter the production is predominantly oriented to agriculture. Soon after Independence, the Government of India launched the process of industrialisation as a conscious policy for economic development in the early fifties. During the colonial rule, lack of infrastructural facilities coupled with the absence of core and basic industries had discouraged entrepreneurship from the private sector to take a lead in the industrial development of the country. Moreover, in the face of unequal distribution of wealth and resources in the economy, the Government could not entirely depend on the private sector to bring about the desired pattern of industrial development. So, to promote industrialisation, the Government of India adopted the concept of a mixed economy wherein the Government and the private capitalists would work with complementarities and competitiveness, leaving the development of key and basic industries in the hands of the public sector. Thus, the public sector enterprises are given the responsibility to :

(i) control the growth of private monopolies,
(ii) accelerate the overall economic growth in the country,
(iii) act as a kingpin for a socialist pattern of development,
(iv) promote balanced regional development,
(v) reduce inequalities in income and wealth,
(vi) generate economic surplus, and above all
(vii) act as an instrument of social transformation.

Since one of the professed objectives of the public sector institutions in the country is to remove regional imbalances and promote balanced growth within the region, it is necessary to study the impact of the public sector on the city and its hinterland. When a public sector project is established in any region, it should get integrated with the regional economy and promote an all round development of the region through its backward and forward linkages and the multiplier effects.

The present study is concerned primarily with the impact analysis of a Bharat Heavy Electricals Limited (BHEL) unit located in the city of Bhopal, the capital of Madhya Pradesh. The construction activities within the BHEL township generated large scale migration of skilled and unskilled people into the city of Bhopal. The population of Bhopal city which was only one lakh in 1951, grew to over six lakh within thirty years. The present city of Bhopal looks like a mini India, as people from almost all the states are present here in large numbers. Several modern industrial units, linked with the BHEL factory, came up within the city as well as in the surrounding areas. This led to enormous physical expansion of the city limits. The vertical and horizontal growth of the city led to significant changes in the socio-economic characteristics in the hinterland as well. Besides, it promoted the growth of a large number of consumer goods industries such as food and beverages, tobacco, wood and wood products, chemicals etc., through multiplier effects, due to the increase in the purchasing power of the workers. Above all, the BHEL unit of Bhopal contributed a lot towards increasing the power generating capacity in the country and, at the same time, earned valuable foreign exchange by exporting heavy electrical equipments. It has generated substantial investible surpluses especially since early seventies and the BHEL corporate sector as a whole is reckoned as one among "the best ten" profit earning public sector units in India.

An analysis of the economics of the BHEL plant, its impact on the city and the regional economy and the changes in its socio-economic characteristics occurring during the past thirty years has been attempted through secondary statistics. In order to examine the impact of the factory on its immediate neighbourhood in some detail, a field survey was carried out in 24 villages around the city. Also, a household level survey was conducted in six selected slums to assess their linkages with the BHEL unit and their changing characteristics.

The present volume owes much of the analysis to a research project sponsored by the Indian Council of Social Science Research to assess the impact of the BHEL unit on the region. The project has been completed under the Directorship of Professor Girish K. Misra in collaboration with Shri Rajkishor Meher during the tenure of their work in the Council for Social Development, New Delhi. Dr Amitabh Kundu was an honorary consultant to the project. The regional analysis in the volume draws significantly from a UGC sponsored study on "Regional Disparities in India", being conducted at the Jawaharlal Nehru University under the overall supervision of Dr. Kundu.

We owe a debt of gratitude to the BHEL personnel of the Bhopal unit, Dr. V.D. Garde, Deputy General Manager (Management Services), Shri S.R. Khan, Deputy General Manager (Public Relations), Shri S. Seshadri, Senior Manager (Personnel) and Shri S. Sethuraman, Deputy Manager (Management Services). We are also thankful to Shri B.S. Baswan, Director of Industries, Madhya Pradesh and Shri B.K. Srivastava, General Manager, District Industries Centre, for their continuing support. Above all, the industrialists of Bhopal and the people of the surveyed villages deserve our special thanks for providing us the required information at the time of the field study. The most satisfying experience during our field visit was our meetings with Mirza Fahim Beg, Ex-Deputy Chief Engineer, P.W.D., Bhopal State who narrated to us the story of BHEL since its inception. His recollections were bereft of statistics but had the warmth of feelings and love for the factory, he had seen growing everyday like a child. He provided insights into the socio-political processes of that time which revealed much more than what an analysis of the scanty data of the fifties could. Last but not the least, the secretarial assistance rendered by Mr. Surendra Pal Sharma in giving the manuscript its present shape is acknowledged.

New Delhi
September 1986

AMITABH KUNDU
GIRISH K. MISRA
RAJKISHOR MEHER

CONTENTS

LIST OF TABLES

LIST OF APPENDICES

LIST OF FIGURES

1

PUBLIC SECTOR AND REGIONAL DEVELOPMENT IN INDIA

INTRODUCTION

The first Industrial Policy Resolution of 1948 proposed the concept of a mixed economy in Independent India wherein the Government and the private capitalists are expected to work together for the rapid industrial development of the country, leaving the key and basic industries with the state sector. The multi-dimensional objectives of the public sector units at the macro level are the following :

(i) To capture the commanding heights of the economy by sharing the burden of the country's industrialization programme ;
(ii) To provide an adequate return on the investments ;
(iii) To generate additional employment and also help in protecting employment in the case of sick industrial units taken over from the private sector ;
(iv) To promote a balanced regional development within the country ; and
(v) To help in the development of ancillary industries, small scale units, etc.

Strategy for regional development in India

In order to analyse the impact of governmental policies on the process of regional development in India, it would be appropriate to review the overall planning process in the country in the context of the Centre-State relationship. It is important to critically examine the attempts made by the Federal Government to sponsor and promote growth in the backward states by providing financial and other assistance to the state governments and also by making direct investment through the public sector undertakings.

The Central Government in India attempts to ensure inter-state balance by transferring funds to states on the basis of certain well-designed formula, based on principles of spatial equity and social justice. Funds are transferred from the centre to the states in two ways—one, as per the recommendations of the Finance Commission for non-plan expenditures and two, distribution of plan funds among the states through the Planning Commission.

A number of scholars have analysed the spatial pattern of the transfer of funds through various Finance Commissions and have generally argued that the backward states were not necessarily the privileged ones in this regard. It has been noted that a few developed and middle level states have received larger transfers in per capita terms (Table 1.1). The rank correlation co-efficients between incomes and transfers (in per capita terms) among the states work out as negative but statistically insignificant. This suggests that the transfers recommeded by the Finance Commissions do not exhibit a distinct bias in favour of the less developed states. The correlation between the per capita income and the percentage of people below the poverty line also gives a similar conclusion. It is observed that Uttar Pradesh and Jammu & Kashmir among the poorer states have been able to obtain larger per capita transfers. It is, however, unfortunate that Madhya Pradesh, the largest and the most backward state of the country has received very small amount by way of transfer of non-plan resources. Thimmaiah (1985) in his study has shown that Madhya Pradesh ranks third or fourth from the bottom in terms of per capita non-plan transfers recommended by the Second to the Seventh Finance Commissions. Madhya Pradesh being a poor state with a small budget could get only a meagre non-plan assistance from the Centre, the per capita receipts being one of the lowest among the states in the country.

The transfer of plan resources through the Planning Commission, does not show any clear pattern (Table 1.2). Relatively developed states like Maharashtra and West Bengal received

TABLE 1.1 : **Devolution of financial resources from the centre to the states on the recommendations of the Finance Commissions**

States	Second Finance Commission (1957-58 to 1961-62)			
	Per cent to Total Assistance	Rank	Per Capita Assistance (Rs.)	Rank
Andhra Pradesh	8.5	5	26.48	8
Assam	4.3	12	42.17	3
Bihar	9.0	4	22.00	13
Gujarat	3.4	14	18.94	15
Haryana	—	—	—	—
Himachal Pradesh	—	—	—	—
Jammu & Kashmir	2.3	15	71.76	1
Karnataka	7.0	6	33.49	4
Kerala	3.6	13	24.31	10
Madhya Pradesh	6.8	8	24.18	11
Maharashtra	10.4	2	30.12	6
Manipur	—	—	—	—
Meghalaya	—	—	—	—
Nagaland	—	—	—	—
Orissa	4.5	11	28.84	7
Punjab	4.9	9	51 13	2
Rajasthan	4.5	10	26.47	9
Sikkim	—	—	—	—
Tamil Nadu	6.9	7	22.68	12
Tripura	—	—	—	—
Uttar Pradesh	13.5	1	20.49	14
West Bengal	9.8	3	32.55	5
Total	1,048.97 (Rs. crore)	—	26.74	—

TABLE 1.1 : (*Contd.*)

States	Third Finance Commission (1962-63 to 1965-66)			
	Per cent to Total Assistance	Rank	Per Capita Assistance (Rs.)	Rank
Andhra Pradesh	9.3	2	33.94	8
Assam	4.5	13	49.33	3
Bihar	7.8	4	22.09	14
Gujarat	6.4	9	41.28	4
Haryana	—	—	—	—
Himachal Pradesh	—	—	—	—
Jammu & Kashmir	1.6	15	61.08	1
Karnataka	6.1	10	34.44	7
Kerala	5.2	12	40.49	5
Madhya Pradesh	6.6	8	26.82	13
Maharashtra	9.1	3	30.22	9
Manipur	—	—	—	—
Meghalaya	—	—	—	—
Nagaland	0.5	16	18.23	16
Orissa	7.7	5	57.67	2
Punjab	4.5	14	29.05	10
Rajasthan	5.3	11	34.83	6
Sikkim	—	—	—	—
Tamil Nadu	6.9	7	27.24	11
Tripura	—	—	—	—
Uttar Pradesh	11.2	1	20.06	15
West Bengal	7.1	6	26.83	12
Total	1,310.76 (Rs. crore)	—	30.39	—

TABLE 1.1 : (*Contd.*)

States	Fourth Finance Commission (1966-67 to 1970-71)			
	Per cent to Total Assistance	Rank	Per Capita Assistance (Rs.)	Rank
Andhra Pradesh	8.1	3	65.08	8
Assam	5.0	11	122.09	4
Bihar	6.8	8	42.51	16
Gujarat	4.2	13	58.91	11
Haryana	—	—	—	—
Himachal Pradesh	—	—	—	—
Jammu & Kashmir	2.2	14	185.62	2
Karnataka	7.4	5	91.33	6
Kerala	6.5	9	111.58	5
Madhya Pradesh	5.6	10	50.05	15
Maharashtra	9.0	2	65.83	7
Manipur	—	—	—	—
Meghalaya	—	—	—	—
Nagaland	2.0	15	2,164.08	1
Orissa	8.0	4	132.12	3
Punjab	2.0	16	28.32	17
Rajasthan	4.5	12	64.70	9
Sikkim	—	—	—	—
Tamil Nadu	7.1	6	61.56	10
Tripura	—	—	—	—
Uttar Pradesh	12.9	1	50.58	14
West Bengal	6.8	7	56.52	12
Total	2,885.86 (Rs. crore)	—	65.68	—

TABLE 1.1 : (*Contd.*)

States	Fifth Finance Commission (1969-70 to 1973-74)			
	Per cent to Total Assistance	Rank	Per Capita Assistance (Rs.)	Rank
Andhra Pradesh	7.9	5	77.99	8
Assam	4.5	11	130.51	3
Bihar	9.5	2	72.79	10
Gujarat	4.2	13	68.75	13
Haryana	1.3	17	59.39	17
Himachal Pradesh	—	—	—	—
Jammu & Kashmir	2.5	14	231.42	2
Karnataka	4.6	10	67.38	14
Kerala	4.5	12	90.61	5
Madhya Pradesh	6.4	7	65.78	16
Maharashtra	8.9	3	76.10	19
Manipur	—	—	—	—
Meghalaya	—	—	—	—
Nagaland	1.8	16	1,562.98	1
Orissa	5.8	8	114.23	4
Punjab	2.0	15	65.80	15
Rajasthan	5.1	9	86.02	6
Sikkim	—	—	—	—
Tamil Nadu	6.4	6	71.63	11
Tripura	—	—	—	—
Uttar Pradesh	14.5	1	70.20	12
West Bengal	8.6	4	83.33	7
Total	4,266.30 (Rs. crore)	—	82.64	—

TABLE 1.1 : (*Contd.*)

States	Sixth Finance Commission (1974-75 to 1978-79)			
	Per cent to Total Assistance	Rank	Per Capita Assistance (Rs.)	Rank
Andhra Pradesh	8.08	4	162.62	12
Assam	4.57	11	248.09	7
Bihar	8.79	2	134.98	14
Gujarat	3.83	13	122.96	16
Haryana	1.26	20	107.16	21
Himachal Pradesh	2.12	15	528.65	5
Jammu & Kashmir	2.42	14	436.62	6
Karnataka	5.00	10	200.99	9
Kerala	3.99	12	117.72	18
Madhya Pradesh	5.66	8	113.39	20
Maharashtra	7.40	5	127.06	15
Manipur	1.33	19	1,007.95	2
Meghalaya	0.91	21	748.03	3
Nagaland	1.41	17	2,188.23	1
Orissa	6.01	6	234.40	8
Punjab	1.76	16	114.09	19
Rajasthan	5.87	7	189.49	10
Sikkim	—	—	—	—
Tamil Nadu	5.60	9	121.11	17
Tripura	1.38	18	718.42	4
Uttar Pradesh	14.05	1	138.96	13
West Bengal	8.56	3	162.73	11
Total	9,608.85 (Rs. crore)		165.32	

TABLE 1.1 : (*Contd.*)

States	Seventh Finance Commission (1979-80 to 1983-84)			
	Per cent to Total Assistance	Rank	Per Capita Assistance (Rs.)	Rank
Andhra Pradesh	7.17	6	294.54	15
Assam	2.44	13	251.77	21
Bihar	10.42	2	322.34	10
Gujarat	4.54	10	289.80	16
Haryana	1.45	17	245.48	22
Himachal Pradesh	1.53	16	764.87	6
Jammu & Kashmir	1.77	15	625.02	7
Karnataka	4.73	8	280.57	17
Kerala	3.63	12	295.04	14
Madhya Pradesh	7.52	5	298.87	13
Maharashtra	8.07	4	280.44	18
Manipur	0.91	20	1,311.01	3
Meghalaya	0.63	21	1,008.65	4
Nagaland	1.13	18	3,341.53	1
Orissa	4.64	9	361.80	8
Punjab	1.98	14	259.93	20
Rajasthan	4.25	11	267.58	19
Sikkim	0.17	22	1,474.(0	2
Tamil Nadu	7.08	7	316.81	11
Tripura	0.94	19	942.64	5
Uttar Pradesh	15.75	1	314.56	12
West Bengal	9.22	3	347.50	9
Total	21,232.97 (Rs. crore)		356.62	

Source : Some of the figures are taken from Thimmaih, G. "Inter-State Disparities in Financial Allocations" in G.P. Mishra and A. Joshi (eds.) *Regional Structure of Development and Growth in India*, Vol. II, New Delhi, Ashish, 1985, pp. 80-87.

TABLE 1.2 : **Central transfers to individual states during plan periods**

States	First Plan 1951-56		Second Plan 1956-61		Third Plan 1961-66	
	Per Capita (Rs.)	Rank	Per Capita (Rs.)	Rank	Per Capita (Rs.)	Rank
Andhra Pradesh	18	10	31	12	61	13
Assam	21	8	35	7	86	4
Bihar	13	14	22	18	47	17
Gujarat	18	9	31	13	54	15
Haryana	—	—	51	3	62	11
Himachal Pradesh	—	—	—	—	62	12
Jammu & Kashmir	30	5	60	1	172	2
Karnataka	23	6	35	8	66	9
Kerala	16	11	28	15	72	7
Madhya Pradesh	22	7	37	6	68	8
Maharashtra	14	22	23	17	42	19
Manipur	—	—	—	—	—	—
Meghalaya	—	—	35	9	86	3
Nagaland	—	—	35	10	209	1
Orissa	50	2	45	4	78	6

Punjab	151	1	51	2	62	10
Rajasthan	35	4	37	5	80	5
Sikkim	—	—	—	—	—	—
Tamil Nadu	13	13	32	11	55	14
Tripura	—	—	—	—	—	—
Uttar Pradesh	13	15	19	19	48	16
West Bengal	39	3	28	16	45	18
India	23	—	30	14	58	13

TABLE 1.2 (*Contd.*)

States	Three Annual Plans 1966-67 to 1968-69		Fourth Plan 1969-74		Fifth Plan 1974-79	
	Per Capita (Rs.)	Rank	Per Capita (Rs.)	Rank	Per Capita (Rs.)	Rank
Andhra Pradesh	44	11	53	19	152	11
Assam	72	3	117	7	230	8
Bihar	33	17	79	12	113	20
Gujarat	36	14	58	17	114	18
Haryana	58	5	76	13	157	10
Himachal Pradesh	—	—	286	5	613	5
Jammu & Kashmir	160	2	363	3	902	3
Karnataka	45	9	57	18	113	21
Kerala	52	7	80	11	145	14
Madhya Pradesh	43	12	83	10	114	19
Maharashtra	28	19	47	22	89	23
Manipur	—	—	255	4	600	6
Meghalaya	72	4	334	4	771	4
Nagaland	388	1	759	1	1663	2
Orissa	45	8	71	15	169	9

Punjab	45	10	72	14	149	12
Rajasthan	58	6	112	8	145	13
Sikkim	—	—	—	—	2062	1
Tamil Nadu	35	15	48	20	122	17
Tripura	—	—	472	2	368	7
Uttar Pradesh	35	16	70	16	143	15
West Bengal	32	18	48	21	104	22
India	41	13	88	9	143	16

Source : Data for the first four plans are taken from the unpublished materials of the Planning Commission. For the Fifth Plan, data have been taken from "Finance of State Governments" *RBI Bulletin*, different issues.

larger per capita plan assistance together with some of the backward states during the Second to Fifth Five Year Plans. It is indeed true that some of the poorer states like Uttar Pradesh, Bihar and Madhya Pradesh have claimed relatively higher central assistance in per capita terms. The correlation coefficient between the per capita income and plan transfers per capita (30 per cent assistance and 70 per cent loans), once again, turns out to be negative but insignificant. There is, thus, no reason to believe that the transfers through the planning process in India have helped the economically depressed states a great deal. Madhya Pradesh, of course, has been able to do somewhat better and its share in the total plan transfers has been more than that in the non-plan transfers. In terms of per capita plan transfers, it is placed just above the national average. However, the difference was not much as may be warranted by the disparity in the levels of development and the resource requirements of the backward states like Madhya Pradesh. The central investments in the public sector units (Tables 1.3 and 1.4) show a remarkable bias in favour of the backward states. In particular, the states with rich mineral deposits and other industrial resources benefitted the most due to these investments as the primary objective was to develop the basic industries through the utilisation of local resources. It is unfortunate that the states like Rajasthan, Jammu and Kashmir, Assam etc., have not been able to attract much central investment. Madhya Pradesh, however, is one of the major beneficiaries next only to Bihar in per capita terms. Up to March 1977, the national level figure of cumulative investment per capita was only Rs. 209 while the amount for Madhya Pradesh was as high as Rs. 358. The ratio of the state to national figure was 1.71 which, however, went down subsequently. The corresponding ratio works out as 1.52 when one considers the cumulative investment up to March 1979.

It is important to mention that the locations of public sector undertakings were decided by the Planning Commission and the concerned ministries on the basis of economic appraisal of the projects with some consideration for balanced regional development. Often, political factors overweighed the formal socio-economic analysis. This generally worked in favour of the developed states who could muster powerful political support. Lately, however, the principle of commercial viability and cost

TABLE 1.3 : **Statewise percentage distribution of employees in central government undertakings, 1981-82**

State	Percent of Employees to Total Employees
Andhra Pradesh	3.72
Assam	2.23
Bihar	22.01
Gujarat	2.28
Haryana	0.59
Himachal Pradesh	0.50
Jammu & Kashmir	0.10
Karnataka	5.80
Kerala	1.39
Madhya Pradesh	12.79
Maharashtra	8.13
Orissa	3.22
Punjab	1.04
Rajasthan	1.64
Tamil Nadu	3.62
Uttar Pradesh	14.76
West Bengal	18.89
Delhi	0.77
Goa	3.10
Other States/U.T.	0.59
Unallocated	2.83
	100.00

Source : *Annual Reports* on the Working of Industrial and Commercial Undertakings of the Central Government (Public Enterprise Survey), 1981-82.

recovery have been considered as extremely important in taking decisions regarding the location and management of public sector units and consequently one notices a perceptible decline in the share of the poorer states in the total investible resources. With increasing concern for achieving the desirable rate of return among the officials in the Finance Commission, Planning Commission and different ministries, one would expect the future investment decisions to be much less in favour of the backward regions than in the past.

There is one more source through which the development

TABLE 1.4 : **Cumulative investment by the central government (in public sector undertakings) in different states as on 31st March, 1979**

States	Per cent of total investment in all States and Union Territories	Rank	Per Capita investment (Rs.)	Rank
Andhra Pradesh	3.3	12	104	14
Assam	2.4	13	210	8
Bihar	18.4	2	453	1
Gujarat	4.9	6	241	5
Haryana	1.4	16	184	9
Himachal Pradesh	0.7	17	287	13
Jammu & Kashmir	Neg.	18	12	17
Karnataka	3.4	11	158	11
Kerala	2.4	13	154	12
Madhya Pradesh	11.8	3	378	2
Maharashtra	6.2	5	167	10
Manipur	—	—	—	—
Meghalaya	—	—	—	—
Nagaland	—	—	—	—
Orissa	4.5	7	280	4
Punjab	2.2	14	222	6
Rajasthan	1.9	15	97	15
Sikkim	—	—	—	—
Tamil Nadu	3.9	9	132	13
Tripura	—	—	—	—
Uttar Pradesh	4.2	8	67	16
West Bengal	6.9	4	218	7
Unallocated and others (including UTs)	21.5	1	—	—
Total All States	15,667.93 (Rs. crore)	—	248	—

Source : Karnataka *Draft Five Year Plan*, 1978-83.

expenditures in different states can be financed both in the public as well as private sectors. That is the institutional fund which includes credits and investments supported by the nationalized commercial banks, development banks including the Agricultural Refinance Development Corporation (ARDC) and the saving agencies like the Life Insurance Corporation (LIC) and

TABLE 1.5 : **Per capita flow of institutional funds during 1973-80 to different states**

States	Commercial Banks				Development Bank funds (Rs.)
	Credit funds (Rs.)	Investment funds (Rs.)	Total (2+3)	Rank	
(1)	(2)	(3)	(4)	(5)	(6)
Punjab	734	42	776	1	78
Haryana	446	74	520	3	113
Maharashtra	618	49	667	2	131
Gujarat	323	69	392	4	219
West Bengal	321	49	370	6	170
Group A	472	54	526	—	129
Tamil Nadu	327	38	365	7	97
Kerala	316	69	385	5	67
Orissa	85	35	120	20	31
Assam	92	40	132	19	35
Karnataka	315	34	349	9	132
Andhra Pradesh	313	30	343	11	59
Group B	244	38	282	—	74
Uttar Pradesh	121	28	149	17	37
Rajasthan	168	51	219	12	60
Madhya Pradesh	111	27	138	18	26
Bihar	83	26	109	21	23
Group C	115	30	145	—	34
Himachal Pradesh	114	61	175	14	58
Jammu & Kashmir	163	74	237	10	77
Tripura	100	49	149	15	17
Manipur	50	91	141	16	5
Meghalaya	55	127	182	13	86
Nagaland	84	280	364	8	35
Group D	125	80	205	—	56
ALL STATES	521	40	561	—	73

Source : Thimmaih, G. "Inter-State Disparities in Financial Allocations" in G.P. Mishra and A. Joshi (eds.) *Regional Structure of Development and Growth in India* Vol. II, New Delhi: Ashish, 1985 pp. 95-96.

the General Insurance Corporation (GIC). Per capita flow of funds (Tables 1.5 and 1.6) from the commercial banks during 1973-80 had been very much in favour of the developed states.

TABLE 1.5 : (*Contd.*)

States	Rank	ARDC funds (Rs.)	Rank	Total institutional funds (Rs.) (4+6+8)	Rank
	(7)	(8)	(9)	(10)	(11)
Punjab	7	87	2	941	1
Haryana	4	123	1	756	3
Maharashtra	2	30	6	828	2
Gujarat	1	27	8	638	4
West Bengal	9	9	14	449	8
Group A	—	35	—	690	—
Tamil Nadu	5	19	11	481	6
Kerala	10	14	13	466	7
Orissa	16	18	12	169	18
Assam	15	6	16	173	17
Karnataka	3	35	4	506	5
Andhra Pradesh	12	45	3	447	9
Group B	—	26	—	382	—
Uttar Pradesh	14	28	7	214	15
Rajasthan	11	26	9	305	12
Madhya Pradesh	17	32	5	196	16
Bihar	18	20	10	152	21
Group C	—	26	—	205	—
Himachal Pradesh	13	8	15	241	14
Jammu & Kashmir	8	1	19	315	11
Tripura	19	2	18	168	19
Manipur	20	8	15	154	20
Meghalaya	6	Nil	—	268	13
Nagaland	15	4	17	403	10
Group D	—	4	—	265	—
ALL STATES	—	28	—	662	—

Punjab, Haryana, Maharashtra, Gujarat and West Bengal are in receipt of high per capita banking finance and these are clearly the relatively developed states in India. The hilly states that are also economically very backward like Himachal Pradesh, Jammu and Kashmir, Tripura, Manipur, Meghalaya and Nagaland rank quite high in terms of the per capita banking loans. The larger states *viz.*, Orissa, Assam, Uttar Pradesh and Madhya Pradesh, however, have fared much worse by this measure. They have received a very small share of the total bank credits which is

TABLE 1.6 : Investment premium, credit-deposit and investment-deposit ratios

(All figures except per capita investment are in percentages)

States	L.I.C. 1978-79				Commercial Banks 1979-80	
	Investment premium	Rank	Per Capita investment (Rs.)	Rank	Credit deposit ratio	Rank
Punjab	42.1	10	11.1	4	75.5	4
Haryana	—	—	14.5	3	100.5	1
Maharashtra	20.6	16	5.9	9	74.3	5
Gujarat	40.9	13	9.5	6	51.5	13
West Bengal	22.5	15	3.3	20	55.4	12
Group A	—	—	6.8	—	67.1	—
Tamil Nadu	41.4	12	5.8	10	78.7	2
Kerala	53.5	8	6.9	7	67.1	9
Orissa	114.5	1	4.0	17	65.0	10
Assam	84.7	3	4.0	16	51.2	14
Karnataka	24.0	14	3.9	18	74.0	6
Andhra Pradesh	51.2	9	5.7	11	68.4	8
Group B	—	—	5.2	—	71.4	—
Uttar Pradesh	56.8	6	4.4	14	46.8	16
Rajasthan	72.3	5	6.8	8	76.0	3
Madhya Pradesh	56.2	7	3.3	21	56.9	11
Bihar	83.7	4	3.6	19	48.9	15
Group C	—	—	4.2	—	52.6	—

Himachal Pradesh	42.1	11.5	4.2	15	36.3	17
Jammu & Kashmir	—	—	10.0	5	28.9	19
Tripura	—	—	4.9	13	69·7	7
Manipur	—	—	5.1	12	29.5	18
Nagaland	84.7	—	38.2	1	28.0	20
Meghalaya	2.7	2.5	27.2	2	16.4	21
Group D	—	17	9.7	—	31.7	—
Grand Total	41.2	—	5.4	—	64.3	—

TABLE 1.6 : (*Contd.*)

	Commercial Banks 1979-80					
	Investment deposit ratio	Rank	Credit investment deposit ratio	Rank	Proportion of bank investments in total state loans outstanding as on March 1979	Rank
Punjab	4.3	21	79.8	11	60.5	8
Haryana	16.7	8	117.2	2	60.6	7
Maharashtra	5.9	20	80.3	10	51.8	16
Gujarat	11.0	14	62.5	17	54.3	14
West Bengal	8.4	19	63.8	16	46.3	21
Group A	7.6	—	74.8	—	—	—
Tamil Nadu	9.1	17	87.9	6	60.0	10
Kerala	14.7	11	81.8	9	55.7	12
Orissa	27.0	5	92.0	5	49.2	18
Assam	22.4	7	73.7	13	48.0	20
Karnataka	7.9	18	82.1	8	60.4	9
Andhra Pradesh	9.7	16	77.9	12	54.9	13
Group B	11.1	—	82.6	—	—	—

Uttar Pradesh	10.7	15	57.8	18	53.2	15
Rajasthan	23.1	6	99.1	4	57.5	11
Madhya Pradesh	13.6	12	70.5	14	49.4	17
Bihar	15.4	9	64.0	15	48.6	19
Group C	13.7	—	66.1	—	—	—
Himachal Pradesh	15.3	10	1.7	21	79.6	3
Jammu & Kashmir	13.1	13	42.0	20	81.2	2
Tripura	34.2	4	103.8	3	73.9	5
Manipur	53.7	2	82.8	7	74.1	4
Nagaland	93.9	1	121.9	1	64.8	6
Meghalaya	37.9	3	54.3	19	92.7	1
Group D	20.3	—	51.9	—	—	—
Grand Total	10.2	—	74.7	—	54.8	—

Source : George, K.K. *Centre-State Financial Flows and Inter-State Disparities in India*, Seminar Paper, 1982.

extremely low, considering their high share in the population of the country. In particular, Madhya Pradesh received bank assistance of Rs. 138 per capita only during these seven years in the seventies which is about one-fourth of the amount of Rs. 561 for the country as a whole and even lower than the average figure for the backward hilly states which is Rs. 205.

The funds received from the Development Banks follow the same pattern. The advanced states have a distinct advantage in obtaining funds from these agencies as Gujarat and Maharashtra have received the maximum per capita bank credits during 1973-80. Madhya Pradesh, however, does not seem to find favour with these banks as its per capita assistance figure happens to be one-third of the national figure of Rs. 73. ARDC funds, fortunately, do not show this bias distinctly except that the Punjab and Haryana have managed to get three to four times the national average in per capita terms. The figure for Madhya Pradesh is comparable to the national figure of Rs. 28 only. In any case, the total amount disbursed by the ARDC constitutes too small a proportion of the total institutional finance to correct the distortions in the distribution of development finance. The per capita investment made by the LIC in different states also exhibits a "commercial banking bias". While Punjab, Haryana and Gujarat come to the top, Madhya Pradesh (M.P.) is at the bottom in terms of per capita investment. The rank correlation between the aggregate flow of funds (per capita) through institutional channels and income per capita is positive and highly significant which substantiates the proposition that relatively developed states have been enjoying larger benefits. This is because the banking agencies and the LIC, in general, support only after satisfying themselves regarding the commercial viability of the project. The spatial variation in the credit-deposit ratio indicates that the credit institutions have succeeded in mobilising a lot of savings from the household sector in the less developed regions and the states and have diverted these to a few nodes and developed states, in response to the forces of the free market.

One can see that although the direct investment made by the Central Government has been larger in the poorer states and the Planning Commission has also attempted to put larger funds at the disposal of these states, the institutional finance has been playing havoc with all the efforts at balanced regional development.

The inter-state distribution of these funds which constitute a large proportion of the total development expenditure in the country has accentuated the spatial imbalance. A large portion of these funds has been cornered by a few developed states—most of these going to one or two large cities within these states. Thus, while the governmental expenditure in the backward states went to the development of basic industries and economic infrastructure, the institutional finance resulted in the multiplier effects leaking out of these states (Table 1.6). Most of the industrial units technologically intertwined with the basic public sector units did not come up within the region but got located in and around a few large cities in the developed states (Table 1.7). This resulted in the truncation of the production complex—the extracting, elementary processing and low valued industries remained in the backward states while the final processing activities with a high component of value-added moved into the developed states. The movement of the institutional capital smoothened this process of lop-sided industrialisation in the country.

Impact of public sector units on the regional economy

Based on the above analysis of the macro economic policies and the spatial pattern of public sector investments, one would infer that one of the proposed aims of the public sector intervention into the industrial scene was to remove imbalances in the country. In accordance with this, a large number of heavy industrial units were located in backward states especially during the fifties and the early sixties. However, due to technical and financial considerations, the policy of balanced regional development could not be followed for the realisation of input-output linkages of the public sector units within the region. When an industrial unit fails to get integrated with the regional economy, it may act as a drag in the process of regional development. The unit may then become exploitative in nature and generate backwash effects, detrimental to small and medium scale industries existing in the region. Attempts should, therefore, be made to integrate the public enterprises with the social and economic structure of the region. Also national level gains without their-spread effect at the regional level may prove disastrous for the long term growth prospect of the national economy itself.

The impact of a public sector unit on the regional

TABLE 1.7 : **State-wise distribution of number of industrial licences issued during 1953-1982, (Figures are percentages to All-India totals)**

States	1953-61	1956-66	1959-66	1967-74	1970-74	1980	1981	1982 (upto Oct.)
Developed								
West Bengal	18.7	16.5	18.0	12.1	10.1	5.0	7.1	5.8
Tamil Nadu	10.0	9.7	8.2	8.0	8.7	7.7	6.7	10.0
Gujarat	7.6	8.9	7.5	10.6	10.7	17.8	16.8	16.4
Maharashtra	27.3	27.4	31.9	28.4	26.7	22.5	24.3	21.7
Punjab	7.3	6.3	7.0	3.3	2.8	3.7	3.5	3.3
Haryana	—	—	–	0.1	0.1	4.2	0.2	1.2
Karnataka	3.8	3.2	3.7	5.1	5.7	8.4	5.2	7.6
Kerala	4.1	3.6	2.2	1.7	1.7	2.3	3.1	2.3
Total	78.8	75.6	78.5	69.3	66.5	71.6	66.9	68.3
Backward								
Andhra Pradesh	2.8	3.3	3.1	4.7	5.1	8.8	8.1	6.6
Bihar	2.9	5.1	3.2	3.8	3.2	0.8	1.4	—
Rajasthan	1.3	1.8	1.6	2.5	2.6	3.1	5.6	3.3
Madhya Pradesh	1.7	2.5	3.9	2.2	2.5	3.7	3.1	2.0

Assam	1.0	0.9	0.8	1.1	1.1	1.0	1.4	—
Uttar Pradesh	7.4	6.7	5.3	8.4	9.5	6.3	5.4	5.6
Orissa	1.3	1.2	1.2	0.8	0.8	1.6	1.0	2.3
Jammu & Kashmir	—	—	—	0.1	0.2	0.2	0.6	0.5
Nagaland	—	—	—	neg.	neg.	N.A.	N.A.	N.A.
Total	18.4	21.5	19.1	23.6	25.0	25.5	26.6	20.3
Himachal Pradesh	0.1	—	—	4.5	5.6	0.4	0.2	1.2
Manipur	—	—	—	neg.	neg.	—	0.2	—
Meghalaya	—	—	—	0.1	0.1	N.A.	N.A.	N.A.

Notes : * Includes figures only for the first half of 1974.
Source : Asthana, P. "Institutional Finance for Industry and Regional Disparities in India", in G.P. Mishra (ed.) *Regional Structure of Development and Growth in India*, Vol. I, New Delhi : Ashish, 1985, p. 360.

economy may be assessed in terms of two different components, *viz.*, (i) direct impact and (ii) indirect impact. The direct impact is mainly in terms of the demand for men and materials generated for the construction and the operation of public sector unit and the value added which is its contribution to the regional as well as national income. The indirect impact may further be classified into two categories *viz.*, (i) multiplier effects and (ii) propulsive effects. The multiplier effects occur in terms of the increase in demand for men and material resources as a result of the increased incomes of the direct beneficiaries of the unit. The propulsive effects of the units would be in terms of generation of activity in the industries linked to the public sector either as supplier of inputs or consumers of outputs. The quantum of impact in the last category depends on the degree to which the product of the public sector unit is amenable to further processing or can be used as an intermediary product in other units. The magnitude of impact experienced by an economy is also a function of the stage of development. A backward economy may not respond to the increased investment due to the supply bottlenecks prevailing in the region.

The materialisation of the multiplier and propulsive effects depends on the extent to which the Government is able to contain the impact within the region by providing the necessary infrastructural facilities in the shape of good roads connecting the cities with their surrounding villages, supply of power, improved agricultural extension activity and irrigation facilities. It would also be necessary to provide servicing facilities for the machinery to be used in the units by arranging training programmes and extending opportunities to local entrepreneurship.

In the case of public sector units in India and their impact on the regional economy, very few systematic works have been done at the micro level. There is little information collected and compiled regarding the impact of such a project on the local economy. Nevertheless, a few micro level studies seem to suggest that though these industrial units helped the growth of the private sector in the country by providing basic inputs or infrastructure, they did not help the development of the regional economy by providing a large number of jobs to the people of the region and also by utilizing its material resources. In the succeeding paragraphs a few case studies have been discussed that throw light on the impact of the location of public sector units on the regional economy.

The study by Satyanarayana and others (1973) suggests that due to the highly mechanised nature of the projects in Kiruburu, Bailadila and Panna, the bulk of the employment generated by the projects was in the skilled category which was occupied by the outsiders, as the rate of literacy among the tribals was very low. In the mines of Kiruburu and Bailadila on Orissa-Bihar border and Panna in M.P., it is only the casual and unskilled workers that came from the local areas. Of course, the region got some indirect benefits due to the development of transport and communication, expansion of trade and commerce, opening of schools and hospitals, provision of safe drinking water facilities etc. Furthermore, these projects generated additional revenues to the state governments in terms of royalty, excise duties, sales tax etc., which constitute a substantial portion of the non-tax revenue of the State.

In Panna diamond mines, it was found that mechanisation led to the deprivation of source of livelihood for many families because of the lack of technical knowledge and mechanised skill. Prior to the mechanisation of the project, cutting and polishing were done in household industries and about 250 families were engaged in this profession. Out of a total employment of 1,426 persons in the Panna Mining Project in January, 1971, only 969 persons were locals, working largely as contingent and casual labourers.

In the study of the Bharat Aluminium Company (BALCO) project at Korba in M.P.,[1] it was observed that the maximum employment opportunities created by the project had gone to the local people of Chhatisgarh region and also the weaker sections of society like scheduled castes and scheduled tribes. Out of 5,607 persons employed in the project in 1979, abou 2,962 persons were from Chhatisgarh who were quite new to industrial culture and 733 persons were from other regions of Madhya Pradesh. Thus, a total of 3,695 persons, i.e., about 66 per cent were from M.P. In the case of category 'D' where maximum pay was upto Rs. 270 per month[2], 69 per cent of the employed were from Chhatisgarh and 86 per cent from M.P. In the combined category of classes 'C' and 'D', where the maximum basic pay was less than Rs. 900 and the selection was mainly on regional basis, 57 per cent of employees came from Chhatisgarh and 70 per cent from M.P. Even in the category of officers, whose selection is done on All India basis, 21 per cent belong to Chhatisgarh and 34 per cent to M.P. Among the trainees, 80 per cent were from Chhatisgarh and 99 per cent from M.P. Similarly, amongst category 'D', 25 per cent and 23 per cent workers belonged to the scheduled castes and scheduled tribes respectively and in combined category of classes 'C' and 'D', 16 per cent were SCs and 17 per cent STs. Apart from that, thousands of people of this region were engaged in Korba project by the contractors and supporting industries.

In a more systematic study sponsored by the Hindustan Steel Limited and conducted by A.N. Sinha Institute[3] on 'Rourekela Steel Plant and its impact on the Regional Economy' it is found that the region or the Sundergarh district where the project is located has a higher per capita income compared to the state of Orissa. Furthermore, the expansion of the services like trade and commerce, transport, communication and others on account of the steel plant, has benefitted the local people as well as the state economy. However, in terms of the class distribution of gains it is found that the people belonging to upper income brackets and land-owning classes have occupied better paid jobs in the steel plant compared to the landless labourers. Similarly, in other private sector industrial units that have grown due to the spread effects of the steel plant, the better paid jobs and regular type jobs have been bagged by the rich land-owning class whereas the landless labourers are employed in very low paid and casual jobs only.

Although the literacy level has risen in recent years in the region and Sundergarh district has a higher literacy rate compared to Orissa State, the agriculture in Panposh tehsil, where the steel plant is located, is in a very backward state. Commercialisation of agriculture has, so far, not taken place. Very few people grow vegetables and other commercial crops by using HYV seeds and chemical fertilizers, despite the irrigation facilities created by the State Government and the existence of a large demand for vegetables and pulses in Rourkela township. Wage rate in agriculture is found to be extremely low compared to the market wage rate in Rourkela. The earnings of the landless labourers are so low that they fall into the hands of money lenders who are mostly the rich landlords. As the farmers are unable to repay the debt and its high interest, they become attached labourers to the landlords at much less than the existing market rate. Again, owing to the steel pricing policy of the Steel Authority of India Limited (SAIL), the forward linkages have not materialised satisfactorily within the region. The development of the ancillary units in the neighbourhood has been retarded as the steel plant does not follow a stable and consistent policy with regard to purchasing of their products. In a nutshell, we can say that although the Rourkela Steel Plant makes a fraction of its purchases from within the region and utilises the existing resources both human and material of the region, it has not been able to bring about an all round development of the region. On the other hand, it has increased the income inequality in the region as the benefits have failed to percolate downwards to the poorer sections of the society. In the matter of location of public sector steel plants in India[4] we find that most of the plants are located in backward areas and are expected to act as catalysts of growth in promoting regional development by exploiting local resources and also by providing gainful employment to people in the region. In the case of Bokaro, an additional achievement has been the employment of persons displaced as a result of acquisition of land for the project who are now one out of every four employees in the plant. The steel plant is also promoting the growth of the industry in the region in a big way and nearly 500 medium and small scale units have come up around the steel township.

In another study of the impact of a public sector unit on the regional economy, Mohammed Mohsin (1964) finds that the establishment of the railway locomotives plant at Chhittaranjan in West Bengal, in fact aroused a feeling of animosity and frustration in the minds of a large section of natives i.e., the Santhals. To a great many of them, the project is responsible for their relinquishing claims over land that had provided them with livelihood for generations together. Further, for them the locomotives plant is a humiliation and betrayal. The Chhittaranjan loco-township was previously composed of eight Santhal villages. But the natives who inhabited these parts are completely uprooted except a few of them who have settled in nearby villages. Despite the extravagant promises which the project authorities are alleged to have made to the natives at the time of acquisition of their lands, it was found that only a few of them were absorbed in the permanent labour force of the plant. Many people in the nearby villages of the project site we are found to be unemployed and idle and the money compensation paid to them was extremely low. Though agriculture is the main source of livelihood in these villages, because of their small holdings and poor soil conditions they cannot support themselves on the products of land for a greater part of the year. They have to seek work in Chittaranjan as casual labourers and also in the collieries nearby. A glance through the report on a preliminary inquiry on the growth of Steel Towns in India[5] further lends support to these observations. As per the report, in all the three cases, i.e., Rourkela, Durgapur and Bhilai, the establishment of Government sponsored plants exhibits a spectacular example of displacement of natives without their subsequent absorption. In a survey of Durgapur Steel township in 1958, Ramakrishna Mukherjee finds that only one in every two hundred households belonged to the local people living previously within a distance of ten miles of the site of the township. Bulk of activities in the township is in the hands of non-natives and non-Bengalis.[6]

The above case studies reveal that a public sector unit makes significant direct as well as indirect impact on the regional economy in terms of employment generation and utilisation of resources. However, the nature of propulsive effects and the multiplier effects has been limited due to the governmental policies in terms of the pricing of industrial products and the lack of adequate incentives from the state governments to develop agriculture and industry integrated with the public sector unit.

In the present study, we have tried to examine the impact of a BHEL (Bharat Heavy Electricals Limited) unit on the regional economy by taking the help of different socio-economic indicators available from the census reports and the publications of the concerned State Government Departments and the BHEL itself. Besides, we have conducted three field surveys viz., (i) survey of selected industrial units, (ii) household level survey of selected slum localities and (iii) village level survey of twentyfour villages located around the BHEL project in Bhopal city.

Theoretical debate on the impact of the public sector unit, on the regional economy would always remain inconclusive and it would be important to conduct empirical studies on the efficiency and functioning of individual public sector units. In the subsequent chapters, we have made an attempt to examine the functioning of one of the major public sector undertakings i.e., Bharat Heavy Electricals Limited, Bhopal in the context of its regional setting.

REFERENCES

1. BALCO (Bharat Aluminium Company), *Lok Udyog*, Dec. 1979.
2. BALCO has four categories of workers *viz*., A, B, C and D. Category A includes Officers and Executives, category B Supervisers, category C Artisans and Clerks and category D comprises Semi-skilled and Unskilled Workers.
3. A.N. Sinha Institute of Social Studies, *Regional Distribution of Economic Benefits arising from a Steel Plant : A Case Study of Rourkela Steel Plant, Ranchi*, Statistical Division, Hindustan Steel Limited, (Mimeographed), 1975.
4. Wadhwan, M.P. "Public Sector Steel Industry in India—Evaluation of Financial and Physical Performance", *Lok Udyog*, November 1979, pp. 21-29.
5. UNESCO Research Centre, Calcutta, 1959.
6. Ramakrishna Mukherjee, "Sociologists and the Social Change in India Today," *Sociological Bulletin*, Vol. XI, March-Sept. 1962, p. 8.

2

BHEL, BHOPAL : A PERSPECTIVE

HISTORICAL BACKGROUND

The idea of establishing a heavy electrical plant in India to meet the power requirements of the country was mooted by the Government long before Independence. According to the findings of the *Advisory Planning Committee*, December 1946 and the recommendations of a *Technical Committee on Engineering Industries of the Industrial Conference*, December 1947, the Government of India appointed a Committee early in 1948 headed by J.C. Ghosh, the then Director General of Industries and Supplies, to explore the possibility of manufacturing Heavy Electrical equipments to meet the requirements of generation, transmission and distribution of power in the country. The Ghosh Committee recommended that a factory for the manufacture of Heavy Power Plants should be immediately planned as a public sector project in collaboration with foreign manufacturers of international repute.

Subsequently, detailed project reports were invited from certain well-known firms in U.K. and U.S.A. In 1949, three firms namely, Associated Electrical Industries (A.E.I.), United Kingdom, International General Electric Company, United Kingdom, and Westinghouse of U.S.A. submitted their project reports out of which Westinghouse was interested to participate only financially by way of a loan covering a long period to meet the overseas expenditure including the dollar requirements and some permanent investments in the factory. After considering these project reports, the exploratory committee recommended the establishment of a factory for the manufacture of 1,75,000

KW of power equipment per year, requiring an investment of Rs. 17.5 crore. But the implementation of the project was withheld due to the prevailing financial stringency in the early fifties.

In 1951, the Government of India introduced the First Five Year Plan to rehabilitate the Indian economy, devastated by the Second World War and the partition of the country, so that rapid economic transformation could take place through the development of industries and agriculture. As energy plays an important role in the development of modern industry and agriculture, the absence of indigenous manufacturing capacity of heavy electricial equipment, required for generation, transmission and distribution of electric power, had restricted the growth rate of the economy. Consequently, the matter of establishing a Heavy Electrical Plant was again taken up by the Ministry of Production with the Planning Commission in August, 1952 for inclusion among the projects in the First Five Year Plan. Accordingly, a sum of Rs. 7 crore was provided out of the lump sum provision of Rs. 50 crore for basic industries and transport. After that, project reports were again invited from the multi-national firms to participate financially as well as technically for the manufacture of heavy electrical equipments. This time four firms showed interest but ultimately only two of these submitted their reports in early 1954. While the project reports were being examined, the production of certain related items in the existing manufacturing units in the country was expanding and the programme of the proposed state factory had to be co-ordinated with the other undertakings in the country. The Government of India, once again, constituted a committee headed by S.A. Gadkary, Consultant (Power), Planning Commission in October 1954 to review the existing position and suggest measures for improvement. The Committee suggested that the manufacture of heavy electrical equipment in the country was essential for the speedy industrialisation as the existing production was only confined to small transformers and motors, that too in very small quantity and the only way to reduce the increasing imports of these equipments and dependency on foreign countries was to establish the proposed heavy power plant.

Finally, the Government accepted the recommendations of the Gadkary Committee and proposals were invited from the foreign firms engaged in this field for technical and financial collaboration. After a scrutiny of the offers received, M/s Associated Electrical Industries (A.E.I.) of U.K. were selected as Consultants for the design and lay-out of Heavy Electrical Equipment Factory and also to render technical advisory service in the operation of that factory. Consequently, an agreement was signed with the A.E.I. on 17 November 1955 and a company with the name Heavy Electricals (India) Limited (HE (I) L) was established on 29 August 1956 under the Indian Companies Act, 1956. As per the terms of the agreement, the Consultants prepared the detailed project report which they submitted in November 1956 and was approved by the Government of India in March 1957.

Site selection and location of the factory

According to the Consultancy Agreement between the Government of India and the A.E.I., the latter was to act as the Consultants to the Government for the "establishment, equipment and operation of one or more factories for the manufacture of heavy electrical equipment". For the construction of the factory, the Consultants were supposed to provide the technical data and render advice to the Government, firstly, on the number of factories to be set up and secondly, on the site of the factories. The Central Government, Ministry of Production requested all state governments to send their suggestions about the location of the factory in their respective states. A questionnaire was prepared by the Technical Consultants in consultations with the Government. This was sent to different states, although it was decided earlier at a Conference of the Consultants and the Negotiating Committee to send this questionnaire only to a few selected states as follows :

1. Madhya Pradesh, Orissa, West Bengal and Bihar which deserved preference according to reports submitted by the A.E.I. in 1949 ;
2. Andhra Pradesh, Karnataka, Tamil Nadu and Uttar Pradesh which had sent representations on the subject (Hyderabad and Travancore-Cochin had also sent representations but it was decided that owing to their distance from the sources of raw materials, location of

the factory would be uneconomic)[1] ;

3. Other states that had been constituted since 1949 and which merited consideration.

According to the suggestions of the Minister of Defence and Minister of Home Affairs, the questionnaire was sent to all the states and union territories, but among them only twenty states and union territories responded to the questionnaire while the seven *viz.*, Ajmer, Coorg, Delhi, Kutch, Manipur, Saurashtra and Tripura, showed no interest.

Meanwhile at a meeting of the Negotiating Committee held on 28 November 1955, it was decided to give prime importance to the location of the factory and the preparation of a suitable training scheme as soon as possible. The Negotiating Committee thought that the Indian experts should examine (in close co-operation with the foreign experts at a later stage) the materials sent by the state governments to determine the most suitable site for the location of the project. The Committee also discussed broadly the policy of the Government regarding the location of heavy industries. It was decided that, besides strictly economic and technical considerations, the Government might take into account considerations such as regional impact of industries and their strategic dispersal. The consensus was that the Technical Consultants should recommend three to four probable sites for the location of the factory based purely on economic and technical factors and that the Government should make a choice from among these, after giving due weightage to the objective of dispersed industrialisation.[2]

The replies to the questionnaire were examined by the Consultants and after taking into account the physical and economic factors for the establishment of a heavy electrical equipment factory including soil, transport facilities, climate, water supply and electricity, they made a preliminary selection of fourteen states which appeared to offer suitable sites. The other six states, namely, Assam, Himachal Pradesh, Pepsu, Pondicherry, Punjab and Rajasthan were, therefore, excluded from further consideration. The experts appointed by the A.E.I. and accompanied by the Indian experts, Gadkary and Azad set out on an inspection tour of the sites in 14 States, *viz.* Andhra, Bihar, Bhopal, Bombay, Hyderabad-Deccan, Madhya

Bharat, Madhya Pradesh, Madras, Mysore, Orissa, Travancore-Cochin, Uttar Pradesh, Vındhya Pradesh and West Bengal. The Consultants, after taking into consideration the economics of production in the shortest possible time with the lowest capital expenditure and shortage of technical personnel, etc. came to the conclusion that there should be one factory only in the first stage of the project.

Criteria for site selection

In looking for a suitable site, the Consultants laid down certain ideal conditions. These were as follows :

(i) The site chosen should be such, topographically as well as geologically, as to enable the construction of heavy engineering workshops containing cranes upto 120 ton capacity and other types of heavy machine tools, without having to spend exorbitant sums on the foundations. Besides, the site should have uniform level, so as to avoid extensive levelling operations or the erection of buildings at different levels.

(ii) The site must also be extensive enough to provide for a township, say of 60,000-70,000 inhabitants.

(iii) The site as a whole must be free from the danger of floods and be capable of being adequately drained of both sewerage and storm water.

(iv) Another vital requirement was adequate supply of water, available in sufficient quantities in nearby places, to meet the requirements of both the factory and township. There must be a guarantee of a maximum supply of 25 cusec ultimately, even though the project and the township would initially require only 15 cusec.

(v) The factory should be situated so as to enable the delivery of raw materials, both indigenous and imported, to be made to the factory at reasonable transport costs. Since much of the materials would have to be imported, easy accessibility to a good port capable of handling a reasonable amount of goods would be an essential requirement, at least, during the early stages of the construction of the factory. This, in turn, would mean that the site should preferably be adjacent to a main railway line having the capacity to handle substantial extra load and providing direct links with collieries, steel producing areas and a good port.

(vi) Transport facilities capable of handling factory output of the order of 15,000 ton a year initially, rising at the peak production level to 30,000 ton a year, would be an essential requisite. Besides, these lines should be capable of carrying a maximum indivisible load of 110 ton. This in itself would narrow down the choice of the site to an area along a main railway line with connections to all parts of the country.

(vii) Power supply of the order of 5,000 KW and if possible an extra supply of 500 KW for the township should be made available for the project.

(viii) A telephone system for establishing communications with the rest of the country must be made available at the factory site. Hence, it would be desirable to establish it near a trunk telephone system.

(ix) In establishing a factory of the type contemplated, adequate attention should be paid to the climatic conditions. The temperature should not be so high as to have an adverse effect on the ability of the worker to put in the maximum effort at work. Violent fluctuations in temperature from day to night are undesirable as these would cause problems in condensation and accurate measurement of the equipments. High humidity should also be avoided, as it might cause breakdown of insulation for high voltage equipments under test or in storage.

(x) The factory should not be set up in a place which is undesirable from the point of view of health. In other words, the site should be free from malaria and other communicable diseases.

(xi) The site should be in an area not liable to suffer from famine conditions and there should be an adequate supply of food to meet the needs of the workers in the factory.

(xii) An important factor to be borne in mind is to avoid conglomeration of heavy industrial units at the project site. The heavy electrical equipment plant should be so situated that there is no danger of its labour being drawn away to other large projects in the vicinity. Hence, the factory should not be located in the hinterland of a steel factory or of some such large industrial undertaking. The "manufacture of heavy-electrical equipment required a different attitude of mind in the workers to that in a steel works". The work practices differ from industry to industry and, therefore, care should be taken to see that no unhealthy practices are introduced into the factory.

(xiii) The site should be within an easy reach of a centre of engineering education with facilities for lectures and meetings of professional institutions, "that would enable the professional engineers employed in the factory to keep in touch with the latest trends and progress in the technology of their specialisation. This factor was all the more important in the case of equipment designers and production methods engineers".[3]

After taking into account the above criteria, the Consultants concluded that the ideal site could be found in the north-eastern India in the regions of West Bengal, southern Bihar or northern Orissa and the sites offered by the state governments in these three "preferred areas" were Durgapur, Barka Khana and Sambalpur respectively. However, it was decided to survey all the fourteen sites proposed by the states before taking the final decision.

At the time of surveying all these fourteen sites, the experts paid attention to the different factors like climate, availability of raw materials, manpower, transportation and communication, marketing facilities etc. The sites inspected were divided into four groups. The first group consisted of three sites in the "preferred area", namely Durgapur in West Bengal, Barka Khana in Bihar and Sambalpur in Orissa. The second group consisted of places like, Naini in Uttar Pradesh, Anuppur Sangham in the then Vindhya Pradesh (now a part of present Madhya Pradesh after the reorganisation of states in 1956) and Kumhari in Madhya Pradesh. The third group included places like, Bairagarh in Bhopal, Bhilsa in M.P. and Antergaon in Northern Hyderabad. The fourth group comprised sites located in the southern region of India, namely, Chinchawad near Poona, Vishakhapatnam in Andhra Pradesh, Avadi in Tamil Nadu, Bangalore in Karnataka and Kallamassery in Travancore-Cochin (presently Kerala).

The inspection of the fourteen sites was conducted over a period of eight weeks—from the second week of December 1955 to the first week of February 1956. After collecting information regarding the fourteen sites offered by the states, the Consultants pronounced that the site of Barka Khana was the best of them. However, the Consultants felt that the site would lose its existing utility value, if any other major industry was established within a distance of 30 to 50 mile. In the second group, the Consultants regarded Kumhari in Madhya Pradesh as an excellent site in many respects and in the third group Bairagarh in Bhopal was considered to be the best as it fulfilled, most of the conditions specified by the Consultants. However, none of the five sites in the fourth group was found suitable for the establishment of the heavy electrical equipment factory as these were at a considerable distance from the sources of raw-materials. So, with due consideration to all the relevant factors, the Consultant's senior most experts, M/s. Main and Beeby recommended on February 18, 1956, three sites on which it was "practicable to establish the Heavy Electrical Equipment Project with a reasonable and early economic success" provided no steel plants were located in their vicinity. These were Barka Khana in Bihar, Bairagarh near Bhopal and Antergaon in Hyderabad. Finally, the Consultants recommendations were examined by Gadkary, Technical Advisor for the project in the Ministry of Production and detailed discussions were held with the Consultants during the third and fourth week of February 1956. At the same time, a number of communications were received by the Ministry of Production from the various states requesting the proposed factory to be located in their states by putting forth various advantages of the sites offered by them. On the basis of the consideration of all these factors, the Ministry of Production recommended to the Cabinet towards the end of February 1956 that the Heavy Electrical Equipment Plant should be located at Bairagarh near Bhopal as Barka Khana, the most preferred site was pretty close to the proposed steel plant in Bokaro (which is only 36 mile from Bokaro). The decision was justified also in terms of the Government's policy of achieving dispersal of industrial development in the country.

On hearing the approval of the site at Bairagarh in Bhopal by the Central Cabinet, the Bhopal Government assured the Government of India of its co-operation and assistance in the construction of the factory and the township. It agreed to extend the following facilities :

(1) Arrangements would be made for the supply of 400 million cubic feet of water till the end of the fifth year and double that quantity subsequently every year. Even at a liberal estimate the factory's requirements and those of the township were not expected to exceed this quantity.

(2) Water would be supplied to the factory and township at their boundary and the concern will be charged the actual cost of delivery. No capital cost for storage, pumping etc., would be charged to the factory.

(3) The factory's (and the township's) requirements of electricity were guaranteed at the generation cost plus the overheads permitted by the Indian Electricity Act. In other words, no profit would be made from the factory in the supply of electricity.

(4) The required land, approximately 10 square mile for the factory and the township, would be given by the State Government free of cost. It would be made available by the end of June 1956. The uncultivated portion of the land which constituted the majority, however, would be handed over almost immediately.

(5) Two acres of land alongside the lake would be given free for the construction of a hostel for accommodating the foreign technical consultants and their families.

(6) The State Government would be responsible for the necessary diversion of the roads adjoining the factory area to suit the factory and the township.

(7) The State Government would improve the link roads from the factory to their junctions on the main Agra-Bombay road and the Saugar-Allahabad-Calcutta road to 'A' standard within five years. This would substantially meet the requirements of the factory in regard to transportation.

(8) The State would assist in the transfer of certain ex-RAF barracks near the factory site, being used as a destitute-home by the Ministry of Rehabilitation, to the factory, for use as a training camp and for housing the building teams. This would assist the

speedy construction of the factory and the township.

(9) The State Government would also assist in the provision of telephone trunk lines required by the factory and township.

(10) The State Government would provide the required amenities outside the factory area—a school and a hospital—at their cost within the factory.

(11) The State Government would further appoint a liaison officer to ensure speedy implementation of these guarantees.

In short the State Government evinced a genuine desire to assist and co-operate with the Government of India in the construction of the factory and the township.[4]

When a detailed survey of the proposed site was taken up for the location of the Heavy Electrical Equipment Project at Bairagarh near Bhopal, it was found that some portions of the land were not suitable for the erection of the factory because the land beneath the surface was of a soft variety and a good deal of expenditure would have to be incurred to prepare suitable foundations for the factory. Consequently, the site originally chosen had to be abandoned and an alternate site was soon discovered at a distance of about 10 mile from the original location.

Land for the project in the new site was 4,500 acre and was made available by the State Government without any cost. The site is about six mile east of Bhopal city and is bordered by two metalled roads, one going from Bhopal to Raisen and the other from Bhopal to Itarsi. The access to the factory proper is from the Bhopal-Raisen road, whereas the main access to the township is from the Itarsi road. At present, the total land acquired by BHEL Bhopal is 5,030 acre, out of which the factory covers 872 acre and rest of the area is occupied by the township. The nearest railway station to the site is Habibganj. A railway siding has been laid from this station into the factory, providing direct rail connection for supplies of incoming raw materials and despatch of finished products. The land given by the State Government for the establishment of Heavy Electrical Equipment Factory has been utilized by the authority as detailed in Table 2.1.

Rephasing of the project

In the middle of 1957, deterioration in the foreign exchange

TABLE 2.1 : **Land utilisation pattern by BHEL, Bhopal**

	Acres
A. *Factory*	
1. Land developed for factory	543
2. Green-belt around factory	109
3. Land reserved for future development	220
Total	872
B. *Township*	
4. Land under residential plots	775
5. Roads	343
6. Parks, open spaces and low land	451
7. Educational institutions, play grounds, commercial building sites, public buildings and religious places	209
8. Agricultural land	1800
9. Vacant land	580
Total	5030

Source : BHEL, Bhopal, *Facts at a Glance*, March 1981, p. 2.

position necessitated a reappraisal of all the development schemes in the Public Sector and the Consultants for the BHEL were asked to phase the scheme into two or more stages, with emphasis on quick return on investment and saving of foreign exchange, without curtailing the total capacity of the project as contemplated originally. The Consultants prepared a revised programme to complete the project in three phases as given below :

(a) Phase I
(1) Production of (i) Switchgears, (ii) Transformers, (iii) Control gears, (iv) Capacitors, to start by the end of 1960.
(2) Full production level to be achieved by January 1965.
(3) Annual output value to be Rs. 6.21 crore.

(b) Phase II
(1) Production of (i) Industrial motors, (ii) Traction motors, (iii) Heavy Electrical Rotating Plants, to start by July, 1963.
(2) Full production level to be achieved by January 1967.
(3) Annual output value to be Rs. 4.16 crore.

(c) Phase III (1) Production of (i) Hydraulic Turbines, (ii) Rectifiers, to start by July 1966.
(2) Full production level to be achieved by July 1970.
(3) Annual output value to be Rs. 2.12 crore.[5]

In the beginning, the Consultants proposed an annual output of Rs. 12.5 crore in a single shift. As mentioned earlier, the foreign exchange crisis of 1957 necessitated a decomposition of the project into three phases and production started in one part of the factory on Ist July 1960. But in the same year the Planning Commission reviewed the country's requirements of heavy-electrical equipments and decided to double the output of the factory to Rs. 25 crore per annum in two shifts working against the original level output of Rs. 12.5 crore. Thus, in order to meet the likely increase in the demand for heavy electrical equipments, the Project Report of the Consultants had to be revised from time to time, covering proposals for expansion of the original product lines viz., switchgears, transformers etc., and also for taking up the manufacture of new product lines, viz. steam turbines and generators. Table 2.2 indicates the estimated cost of the project as envisaged in the Project Report prepared in November 1956 *vis-a-vis* the revisions made from time to time and expenditure incurred by the company on them upto 31st March 1969.

According to the Report of the Committee on Public Sector Undertakings, 5th Lok Sabha, 1972, the revised cost estimate, with the expansion in various schemes including that in the township was to reach Rs. 82 crore for an ultimate output of over Rs. 60 crore per annum.[6] As per the recent data, the BHEL unit at Bhopal incurred a total expenditure of Rs. 89.37 crore upto 31st March 1980 on the factory and the township. The unit was able to produce a total cumulative finished output of Rs. 1,374 crore till the year 1980-81 since its inception in 1960-61.[7]

Construction of the factory

After signing the agreement with the Consultants, the construction of the Heavy Electrical Equipment Factory and township at Bhopal was started by the Government of India on first December 1957 and the Chief Managing Director of construction work

TABLE 2.2 : **Estimated cost of BHEL unit**

Sl. no.	Particulars	As per project report (Nov. '56) Output Rs. 12.5 Crore	1st Revision (Dec. '62) output Rs. 25 Crore	2nd Revision (Sept. '63) output Rs. 25 Crore	3rd Revision (April '66) output Rs. 33.65 Crore	4th Revision (Feb. '70) Output Rs. 33.65 Crore	Actual expenditure up to 31st March '69
(1)	(2)	(3)	(4)	(5)	(6)	(7)	(8)
1.	Factory building and works	1,136	1,331	1,338.60	1,338.60	1,338.60	1,313.85
2.	Factory services	339	405	407.57	491.80	491.80	527.98
3.	(a) Plant and machinery	1,851	1,851	2,082.75	228.86	2,378.75	2,296.31
	(b) Custom duty	—	90	100.57	268.28	389.00	368.59
	(c) Purchase agency agreement and credit agreement	—	113	—	—	—	—
4.	Lump sum payment to Consultants	54	54	53.32	60.02	60.02	59.38
5.	Cost of U.K. training	100	100	100	124.76	124.76	124.76
6.	Furniture and miscellaneous equipment	45	45	45.41	48.72	48.72	53.31
7.	Permanent hostel for trainees	—	41	—	—	—	—

8. Township	—	900	839.92	836.41	839.00	836.65
9. Administration charges	—	—	144.14	290.41	299.41	300.65
10. Payment of interest	—	—	5.27	90.55	90.55	81.31
11, Construction of stores	—	—	—	—	50.00	46.21
12. Block X	—	—	4.00	—	—	—
Total	3,525	4,930	5,121.55	5,847.41	6,110.61	6,009.00

Source : *Committee on Public Undertakings (COPU)*, 19th Report, Fifth Lok Sabha, 1972, pp. 17-18.

was S. Sarangpani. Mirza Fahim Beg was taken as the Deputy Chief Engineer on deputation from the State Government. In course of time, the construction activities took the shape of a complete civil department with thirteen divisions whose chief executives were all engineers by profession.

There were many contractors and sub-contractors engaged in the construction activity of the factory and the township to expedite the work. The chief agencies were : B.B.J. Jessop and Company, Richardson and Cruddas, Tirathram and Company, Uni-Steel, Larsen and Toubro, Dalmia Construction Company, Akal Corporation, Takhtmal Sethi Company, A. Wahid and Company, Shukla and Company, Sindh Construction Company, Talwar and Company, Jain and Company, Jaimiller Company, Jaiprabesh Mallik and others. At that time, the Chief Executives of the civil divisions were, Mirza Fahim Beg, B.S.N. Wadhva, and B.K. Lakshminarayan.

In the construction of the factory and the township, the materials used were supplied by different agencies from different parts of India and abroad. The steel used in the factory and the township was supplied from the Bhilai Steel Plant, cement from the Cement Factory at Bilaspur, bricks, black stone and wood came from the local area within a radius of 15-20 km, asbestos and aluminium sheets from Hyderabad and Kanpur, marble stone from Makarana, Jabalpur and Agra and glasses and other materials from various places outside Bhopal. Besides, 10 per cent of the bricks of special type came from Itarsi and Kanpur. The bricks used in the Administrative Block were brought from Kanpur. The wooden furniture used in the factory block and township were made in Bhopal and supplied by the local agencies like Kazi, Zalil and others and the steel furniture were supplied by Khira and Godrej Company.

The labour engaged by these companies in executing the construction of different blocks of the factory, came from different parts of India recruited by their own agencies. According to A.H. Khan, a senior Manager of BHEL, Bhopal, who was earlier associated with the construction activities of the factory, "95 per cent of the workers engaged in the construction of the factory were brought from outside and only five per cent from the local area as special skill was necessary for the erection of the factory blocks. However, most of the labourers and sub-contractors engaged for the development of the township were from the local area".

The M.P. Government had promised the requisite supply of water and electric power for the factory and township from Bhopal lake and Chambal Grid over a 132 kV line terminating at Bhopal. As no such arrangement was made at that time, power requirements for the construction activities were being met from the local thermal power station at Bhopal.

Under the revised phasing of the project, factory Blocks I and II were initially omitted and two-thirds of Block-III, the whole of Block-IV and half of Block-V were constructed in the beginning. But in view of the Government's reappraisal of the additional electric power generation capacity to be provided during the Third and Fourth Five Year Plans, it was decided to take up Phases II and III along with Phase I and to build up part of the Factory Block-III which was not included in Phase I. The entire work of design, fabrication and erection of the main factory blocks III, IV, V and the Maintenance Block was entrusted to M/s Braithwaite Burn and Jessop Construction Company Ltd., Calcutta.[8] Contract for the execution of the structural steel work of Blocks I and II was awarded to M/s Richardson and Cruddas of Bombay in February 1960 at an estimated cost of Rs. 143.50 lakh inclusive of the sales tax.[9]

Simultaneously, the construction work in the township was going on smoothly. During 1959-61, 4,525 quarters were constructed in the township and it just took four hours on an average to build a quarter. In the year 1961-63, about 3,323 quarters were constructed in different sectors of the township. This implies that it took only five hour and 16 minute on an average to build one quarter. Again, during 1963-65, 1965-66 and 1967-69 about 2,142, 584 and 780 quarters respectively were constructed.[10] Clubs, welfare centres, schools, dispensaries, temples, cultural centres, shopping complexes etc., were also built in the township for the benefit of its employees. One guest house and one field hostel were also built for the customers and guests. One training school and a workshop well-equipped with machine tools, similar to the one to be installed in the main factory, to impart training to about 900 trainees in single shift and to 1,800 to 2,000 trainees in double shifts were also constructed. Besides, one 12 M.G.D. (million gallon per day) water filtration plant, two sewerage plants of one M.G.D. and 0.5 M.G.D. were constructed. A few other facilities were also provided for the benefit of the people in the township. Among them are the 118 mile long road net works, 131 mile long undergrounds sewage pipelines, 102 mile long drainage pipes of various sizes, 72 mile long electric lines and the two mile long service tunnels.

All the ten blocks were constructed to serve different needs of the Heavy Electrical Equipment factory at a cost of 1,176.4 lakh of rupees at current prices. Block-I was meant for Hydro-turbine, Block-IA for fabrication, Block-II for Heavy Rotating Equipment like turbogenerator industrial motor and traction motor, Block-III for manufacture of transformers and capacitors, Block-IV for switchgear and control gear, Block-V for foundry, Block-VI for steam turbine. Block-VII was for storage of machinery and equipment and for the maintenance of assets within the factory. There is yet another Block, known as the Administrative Block. Table 2.3 provides the information regarding the area of each block and the amount spent on the construction of each block at the current prices.

TABLE 2.3 : **Block-wise area and construction cost of BHEL, Bhopal**

Block	Area of the Floor	Construction Cost Rs. lakh
Block-I	4,32,000 c. ft.	221.00
Block-IA	1,28,000 c. ft.	44.00
Block-II	4,56,000 c. ft.	252.00
Block-III	4,44,680 c. ft.	202.40
Block-IV	3,34,000 c. ft.	166.12
Block-V	1,32,000 c. ft.	47.00
Block-VI	1,28,000 c. ft.	169.00
Block-VII	1,00,000 c. ft.	30.00
Maintenance Block	33,000 c. ft.	14.37
Administrative Block	1,00,000 c. ft.	30.85
		1,176.74

Source : *Sandesh*, BHEL, Bhopal, November, 9, 1973.

To save foreign exchange, a survey of indigenous machine tool manufacturing capacity was made with the help of an expert deputed by the Consultants and it was estimated that about 20 per cent of the total requirements of machine tools and equipments could be obtained from within the country. Items not available within the country were purchased from abroad and financed out of the bank credit provided by a Syndicate of London Banks arranged by the Consultants.[11] The work of supply and erection of electric overhead travelling cranes was awarded to Jessop & Co., but that of jib cranes and lifting beams were awarded to indigenous manufacturers. Precision milling machines and lathe machines were supplied by the H.M.T., Bangalore.

Beginning of production and the range of products

The foundation stone of Heavy Electrical Equipment Factory, Bhopal was laid down by late Shri Lal Bahadur Shastri, Minister for Heavy Industry on the 15th of November 1958 and it was formally inaugurated by the then Prime Minister, Pandit Jawaharlal Nehru on 6th November 1960. After the completion of Block-IV on 6th November 1960, production was started in the factory and the first product to come out of the factory was in July 1961. Table 2.4 gives a production profile of the first unit of Heavy Electrical Equipment Plant at Bhopal.

At present the product basket of BHEL, Bhopal includes : (1) hydro sets consisting of hydro turbines of Kaplan, Francis and Pelton types with matching generators, valves and auxiliaries and reversible pump storage sets, (2) thermal sets comprising steam turbines up to 210 MW, nuclear turbines of 236 MW, marine turbines with matching condensors and heat exchangers, (3) transformers ranging up to 400 kV of power transformers, instrument transformers and reactors, (4) switchgear comprising indoor metal clad oil circuit breakers for 11 kV applications, and outdoor oil circuit breakers up to 33 kV, (5) bus duct up to 22 kV voltage rating and 10 kV normal current, (6) control gear for industrial application with oil vacuum contractors, traction control gear equipment for railways and other traction applications, control relay panels for power stations and transformer tapchangers applications, (7) capacitors up to 400 kV system of medium and high voltage, non-PCB capacitors, coupling capacitors up to 400 kV class and surge capacitors for protection, (8) electrical machines and industrial machines consisting of A.C. induction motors, A.C.

synchronous and synchronous induction motors, D.C. general purpose machines, D.C. exciters, D.C, mill motors, D.C. large machines and amplidynes, (9) traction equipment and manufacture of electric trolley buses and battery powered road vehicles and (10) rectifier, thyristor, electronic equipment, etc.[12]

TABLE 2.4 : **Production profile of the first unit of BHEL, Bhopal**

Product	Year of Production
Capacitor	July 1961
Transformer	November 1961 (33 kV for MPEB)
Switchgear	December 1961 (11 kV for MI & AEI, Calcutta)
Traction Motor	January 1963 (for Railways)
Industrial Machine	March 1965 (for M/s Agarwal Hardware, Calcutta)
Turbo Generator	August 1967 (30 MW for Basin Bridge, Madras)
Rectifier	July 1969 (for Union Carbide, Bombay)
Steam Turbine	April 1970 (30 MW for Basin Bridge, Madras)
Water Turbine	May 1970 (Obra Project, UPSEB)
Naval Turbine	March 1975 (for Navy)
Nuclear Turbine	March 1975, 236 MW (for MAPP)

Source : *BHEL, Bhopal at a Glance*, February, 1983.
Note : Against every item the name of buyer is given within brackets.

BHEL Bhopal started production in 1960-61 as mentioned above, with an output of Rs. 0.21 crore and till the year ending 1980-81, it reached a cumulative finished out-turn of Rs. 1,374 crore.[13]

The merger of HE(I) L, Bhopal with BHEL

Till November 1964, three new Projects, (1) Heavy Electrical Plant at Ranipur, Hardwar, (2) Heavy Power Equipment Plant at Ramachandrapuram, Hyderabad and (3) High Pressure Boiler Plant at Tiruchirapalli were being managed by the same company. But due to increasing activities of HE(I) L, Bhopal a new company named Bharat Heavy Electricals Limited BHEL with its head office at New Delhi was incorporated on 17

November 1964 to take over the management of the three new units mentioned above.

In spite of the impressive production built-up as may be seen from the statistics presented in the following sections, the financial affairs of the HE(I) L were causing concern among the employees, the customers i.e. the Electricity Boards, the general public and the Parliament. By 1971, the cumulative loss suffered by the HE(I) L, Bhopal came to Rs. 59.87 crore which reinforced the general dissatisfaction about it and the impression that something was wrong with the unit.[14] Consequently, the Government of India examined in detail the the financial structure of the Company through the Bureau of Public Enterprises under the Ministry of Finance. Later, a High Power Action Committee was appointed to look into the affairs of, among others, the HE(I) L, Bhopal.

After examining the performance of the unit in detail, the High Power Action Committee suggested the merger of the two companies *viz.*, HE(I) L and BHEL

(i) to ensure optimum utilisation of the available resources and expertise.
(ii) to bring about "a high degree of interaction and co-ordination between the plants, so essential in the phases of technology absorption and production." and,
(iii) to achieve integrated working of different heavy electrical units to provide better services to the customers.

Consequently, the Heavy Electricals (India) Limited, Bhopal was merged with the Bharat Heavy Electricals Limited with effect from 1 January 1974 with the accounts merged with effect from 1 April 1973. With this merger, BHEL's total outlay stood at Rs. 238 crore, an equity capital of Rs. 130 crore and loans of Rs. 108 crore in the year 1974-75.[15]

Growth of BHEL, Bhopal

The Heavy Electricals (India) Limited was formed on 29 August 1956 under the Indian Companies Act, as mentioned above. In the beginning of 1957, the Company had a total manpower of 94 which crossed 12,000 mark in the year 1963. It reached the figure of 18,776 at the time of merger of HE(I) L with BHEL in 1974. The strength of the unit on 24 January 1983 was 19,136 workers.

Production also increased very fast since its beginning on the 6th of November 1960. During the year 1960-61, the output was only Rs. 0.21 crore but by the year 1968-69, it had crossed Rs. 25 crore. Again by 1974-75, a major milestone of Rs. 100 crore output was crossed and by the end of the year 1981-82, BHEL, Bhopal registered an out-turn of Rs. 198 crore.

Table 2.5 gives a clear picture of the growth and production performance of BHEL, Bhopal since its inception to the year

TABLE 2.5 : **Growth and production of BHEL, 1960-61 to 1981-82**

Financial year	Total output (Rs. in lakh)	Per cent increase in output	Total manpower	Per cent increase in manpower	Output per employee
1960-61	—	—	1,858	—	—
1961-62	13	—	3,743	101	347
1962-63	144	1,008	7,476	100	1,926
1963-64	470	226	10,852	45	4,331
1964-65	633	35	11,394	5	5,556
1965-66	827	31	12,433	9	6,652
1966-67	1,249	51	13,227	6	9,443
1967-68	1,607	29	14,605	10	11,003
1968-69	2,733	70	14,968	2	18,258
1969-70	1,990	—27	15,240	2	13,058
1970-71	2,945	48	15,504	2	18,995
1971-72	3,827	30	15,845	2	24,153
1972-73	5,525	44	16,301	3	33,894
1973-74	6,976	26	17,303	6	40,317
1974-75	10,227	47	18,776	8	54,468
1975-76	12,697	24	19,055	1	66,633
1976-77	13,638	7	19,074	0.1	71,500
1977-78	11,734	—14	18,988	—.004	61,797
1978-79	12,090	3	18,817	—.009	64,250
1979-80	12,801	6	19,290	2.5	66,361
1980-81	15,561	22	19,298	0.04	80,635
1981-82	19,806	27	19,298	0.00	1,02,632

Source : 1. *BHEL, Bhopal, Facts at a Glance*, March, 1981
2. *Personnel Department*, BHEL, Bhopal.

1981-82, through various indicators like total output, output per employee, per cent increase in output, manpower etc.

It can be seen that the production in BHEL, Bhopal unit has been increasing steadily except during the years 1969-70 and 1977-78, when it showed a negative growth of 27 and 14 per cent, respectively. The percentage increase in manpower has always remained far below the percentage increase in production. This may be taken as a positive indicator of performance of the factory from the efficiency point of view. Of course, the rate of increase in employment in the factory has started going down after 1963-64 and the work force has become more or less stagnant since 1975-76. BHEL, Bhopal is a capital intensive-industry, where the avenues for expanding employment is limited. We cannot blame it for its failure in providing increased employment. On the other hand, it can be argued that the BHEL, Bhopal has been able to increase its production steadily after 1975-76 without any substantial increase in its manpower, as indicated by the data on total output and employees.

Of course, the BHEL, Bhopal was incurring net losses till the year 1972-73 and the total cumulative loss of the factory amounted to Rs. 59.87 crore by the year 1971. Nevertheless, we cannot blame BHEL, Bhopal for its poor performance as the industry was in its infancy and it was manufacturing a wide range of products—steam turbine/water turbine with matching generators on one extreme to small products like capacitors, control gears, small motors, etc., on the other "under one roof and one management". This product mix not only added to the "onerous task" of managing the Bhopal factory but also delayed the profitability of the industry as the gestation period of some of the bigger products varied from 3 to 4 years".[16]

Moreover, according to the detailed report submitted by the Consultants, M/s Associated Electrical Industries, U.K., the project was expected to incur losses from the very inception up to 1970 and that those losses had been provided for in the operating results included in the detailed Project Report and had been accepted by the Government of India. As per the Project Report, the losses up to the year 1970 were expected to be around Rs. 32 crore. Tables 2.6 and 2.7 together provide a comparison of original estimates with the actual performance of production in BHEL, Bhopal during the first five years.

TABLE 2.6 : Original production estimates for the first five years of BHEL, 1960 to 1964

(Rs in lakh)

Production	Year	Output (estimated)	Loss (estimated)	Per cent loss to output
1st Year	1960	63.84	225.33	353
2nd Year	1961	146.87	313.62	213
3rd Year	1962	249.64	385.07	154
4th Year	1963	404.81	434.00	107
5th Year	1964	627.56	362.80	58

Source : 10th HE(I) L, *Annual Report* 1965-66, p.5.

TABLE 2.7 : Actual production performance during the first five years of BHEL, 1961 to 1966

Production	Year	Output at realise-able value	Loss for the year	Adjust-ment relating to prior period	Total	Per cent loss to out-put
1st Year	1961-62	107.52	106.78	10.59	117.37	109
2nd Year	1962-63	310.60	433.57	25.17	458.74	147
3rd Year	1963-64	529.72	568.75	20.06	588.81	111
4th Year	1964-65	610.97	747.61	6.89	754.50	123
5th Year	1965-66	1019.30	674.80	—40.69	634.11	62

Source : 10th HE(I) L, *Annual Report* 1965-66, p. 5.

From the data presented in these tables one can note that though the actual amount of loss incurred during the first five years of production is higher than the estimated loss by the Consultants, the percentage of loss to output has generally not been substantially higher than the estimated figures. We can say that the amount of loss has been higher than estimated largely because the total output during the first five years of production has always been higher than the estimated figures. Besides, the shortfall in achievements can be attributed to the following additional factors :

1. Sophistication, high quality and standard of the

products, the acquisition of the required expertise etc., took a long time and a number of teething troubles were experienced in early years ;

2. indigenous development of materials and components took a long time and few of the suppliers of materials and components failed to keep their delivery commitments including the foreign suppliers and Consultants ;
3. the shortage and non-availability of certain materials led to higher production cost ; and,
4. dependency on foreign suppliers for spares and components in the early years of production increased as there was very little scope for import substitution.

Export promotion and import substitution

The Heavy Electrical Equipment Factory of BHEL (Bhopal) produces heavy electrical equipments not only for domestic consumption but also for the outside market. In order to promote exports, an Export Sales Division was opened in 1968 in BHEL, Bhopal. But the Consultancy agreement with M/s AEI, U.K. prohibited export promotion activities of HE(I)L to Burma, Sri Lanka, Nepal and Pakistan till November 1970 and towards the end of 1970 the restriction was extended to Thailand and Cambodia for certain products only.

The HE(I)L, Bhopal entered into the export market in 1968-69 with an order from U.A.R, worth Rs. 2.73 lakh. By 1974-75 the cumulative order for exports executed by BHEL, Bhopal reached Rs. 1.37 crore and in 1977-78, it had reached a level of Rs. 14.37 crore. In the year 1981-82 alone, exports worth Rs. 8.89 crore were executed and the cumulative exports reached Rs. 59.39 crore. The heavy electrical items exported by BHEL, Bhopal are motors, controls and capacitors to Arab Republic, Singapore and Ghana; switchgears to Iraq; tap changers to Malaysia and micanite sheets to the U.S.A. and Switzerland. The major contracts executed by BHEL in foreign countries cover not only the manufacture and supply, but also the installation and commissioning of power plants like turnkey contract for 2×120 MW Thermal Power Station in Libya and exports of six diesel generating sets with transformers and controls to Saudi Arabia, hydro generators of 8×53 MW and 2×60 MW to New Zealand, 3×29 MW hydro turbines and 1×115 MW hydro generators to Thailand, 2×30 MW hydro generators to Nepal, 3×23 MW hydro sets to Malaysia, 4×30 MVA and 2×20 MVA power transformers to Tanzania and 4×84 MW hydro sets to Bhutan.[17]

Since the beginning of its production, BHEL, Bhopal tried its best to reduce the import content in the manufacture of heavy electrical equipments. In the year 1962-63, the imported raw materials and components were 40.2 per cent of the sale value of the finished products. The high incidence of imported raw materials in production was mainly due to the non-availability of the required items in the home market. Consequently, numerous schemes for the development of the indigenous production of items like transformer-steel, paper insulated conductors, press boards, steel and non-ferrous alloys etc., were initiated through the development of ancillaries and other small and medium scale units in the country. In 1964-65, an Import Substitution Cell was formed to channellise indigenous sources of supply and it concentrated mainly on large value items like steel forging gear, insulation materials, non-ferrous castings, precision steel castings, alloy steel etc., relating mainly to traction, transformer, switchgear and industrial machine equipment. As a result of this, during the year 1966-67, a total saving of Rs. 44 lakh in the c.i.f. value of the imports was made by the Cell and its work was extended to new range of products like hydro and thermal turbine, generator, alternator and large motor and a large number of other items such as pipes, valves, instruments, switches, seals and springs that were to be replaced by indigenous materials gradually. Thus, with the growth of supporting industries and sustained effort made by the BHEL, the over all import content in the cost of production came down from 24 per cent to 19 per cent during 1977-81 as may be observed in Table 2.8.

At present the major items being imported by BHEL, Bhopal are : electrical sheets steel, special grades steel, copper conductors, insulating cables and magnet wires, castings/forgings of larger sizes, special insulating materials and certain other components/proprietory items. The major countrics who supply these items are U.K., U.S.A., West Germany, Japan, France, Switzerland, Austria, Norway and Italy.

TABLE 2.8 : **Trends in the import component to the cost of production**

Year	Percentage of imports to the cost of production
1977-78	23.72
1978-79	21.62
1979-80	21.27
1980-81	17.42
1981-82	11.84

Source : BHEL Bhopal, *Facts at a Glance*, February, 1983, p. 12.

BHEL, Bhopal Today

The Bhopal unit of Bharat Heavy Electricals Limited has grown into one of the largest units in the world for manufacturing heavy electrical equipments producing a diverse range of products starting from small capacitors, control gears and small motors to the manufacturing of bigger and complicated products like steam turbines, water turbines, etc. Till the year ending 31st March 1981, it has designed, manufactured and supplied sophisticated heavy electrical equipments valued over Rs. 125 crore covering the complete range of generation, transmission and utilization of power. It has contributed cumulatively a sum of Rs. 6,557.26 lakh towards interest on Government loans, Rs. 4,181.82 lakh and Rs. 16,218.31 lakh towards excise and custom duties respectively and Rs. 3,582.48 lakh towards sales tax, up to March 1981.[18]

The unit's accomplishment is not merely limited to the production of equipments. Since its inception, it has laid due emphasis on the human resources and developing a modern and healthy industrial community—a real asset for the Nation. The township developed by BHEL, Bhopal has become a mini city within a city covering a population of 1,25,000, a land area of 20.3 km^2 and 12,054 residential quarters of different types. The township is equipped with almost all modern facilities, *viz.* one hospital with 350 beds, nine peripheral clinics, 13 shopping centres, seven banks, five post offices, 44 educational institutions including two degree colleges, 34 recreation, social and cultural institutions, 20 religious institutions, three parks and a plantation of six thousand trees to make the township green and pleasant.

The water to the factory and township is supplied from the

Upper Lake in Bhopal city conveyed through 914.40 cm diameter pipeline to BHEL filtration plant, capable of supplying filtered water at 8.25 mgd. To augment and to have an alternative source of water supply in case of emergency, tubewells have been dug and tanker arrangement has been made for the township. In addition, four storage reservoirs of 5.7 mgd capacity at the filtration plant and eight overhead tanks of one lakh gallon capacity each and one tank of 0.5 lakh gallon capacity have been constructed in various neighbourhoods of the township. The entire sewage and effluent from the township and factory blocks are conveyed through the sewage pipes of various sizes covering a length of 192 km. The sewage is treated in two sewage treatment plants of the company before being disposed off into the rivers and streams and the adjacent land. Electricity is supplied by the Chambal Hydel Project and distribution is made through the 18 distribution centres of BHEL with a connected load of about 14,000 KW.

Cultural activities in the township are being looked after by the Bharat Heavy Electricals Cultural and National Integration Samiti (BHECNIS) formed by BHEL Management to promote social and cultural activities and help the process of national integration. There are 17 cultural associations representing various states and languages of India affiliated to this BHECNIS. These associations organise different festivals, dances and dramas at different times throughout the year in which people belonging to different regions, communities and languages participate. Various types of facilities like health, education, banking, post, telegraph etc., are made available to all the BHEL employees irrespective of grade and status. These services, excepting the medical facility are also extended to the people living in the neighbouring areas.

In nutshell, we may say that the BHEL, Bhopal is a living symbol of a well-knit industrial community—"a mini India", where people belonging to different regions, languages and communities live together in a harmonic social environment without any sign of regionalism, lingual conflicts, communalism or ethnocentrism.

REFERENCES

1. Khera S.S., *Establishment of the Heavy Electrical Plant at Bhopal*, (New Delhi : IIPA, 1963), p. 80.
2. ibid., p. 81.
3. ibid., pp. 82-85.
4. ibid., pp. 111-113.
5. Second Annual Report, HE (I) L, 1957-58, pp. 6-7.
6. *Committee on Public Undertakings*, (COPU), 19th Report, Fifth Lok Sabha, 1972, p. 18.
7. *BHEL, Bhopal*, March 1981, p. 3 and 7.
8. IIIrd HE(I) L, *Annual Report* 1958-59, p. 3.
9. *Sandesh*, BHEL, Bhopal, November 9, 1973.
10. ibid.
1. IInd HE(I) L, *Annual Report*, 1957-58, p. 11.
12. *BHEL, Bhopal at a Glance*, February 1983. pp. 5-7.
13. ibid, p. 7.
14. Naidu, W.G., A Study in depth of some aspects of Management of HE(I) L, Bhopal, Nagpur University, 1980 (Ph. D. Thesis), p. 19.
15. *Annual Survey of Industrial and Commercial Undertakings of Central Government*, 1974-75, Vol. II, p. 72.
16. Naidu, W.G., op. cit. p. 20.
17. BHEL, Bhopal, *Facts at a Glance*, February 1983, pp. 7-8.
18. BHEL, Bhopal, *Facts at a Glance*, March 1981.

3

FINANCIAL VIABILITY OF BHEL—A COMPARISON WITH PUBLIC SECTOR ENTERPRISES IN INDIA

The Industrial Policy of Independent India which was first announced in 1948 envisaged a mixed economy with an overall responsibility of the Government to direct the economy towards certain social and economic goals. To capture the "commanding heights of economy, and to bring about rapid industrialisation" the Government of India took initiative in developing key and heavy industries in the public sector, as the private sector in India did neither have the appropriate entrepreneurial base nor the required capital to come into these industries.

Till the end of March 1981, India had invested Rs. 21,216 crore in 185 enterprises from a meagre amount of only Rs. 29 crore in five enterprises at the commencement of the First Five Year Plan in 1951. Presently, the public enterprises in India are operating in diverse fields starting from industries like steel, heavy and light engineering, fertilizers and basic chemicals, drugs, mining and minerals, petroleum and ship building to service sectors like transport, communication and banking. In 1977-78, the public sector accounted for 65 per cent of the employment in the organized industrial sector and emerged as a catalyst in building the national economy. It is thus clear that the public sector is playing a dominant role in determining the pace and pattern of economic growth in India.

It has been mentioned above that till the year 1972-73, the factory in Bhopal was incurring net loss and the total cumulative loss of the factory had risen to Rs. 67.40 crore. But with its merger with BHEL in 1974, the Bhopal unit has been earning net profit that amounted to Rs. 807 lakh in 1974. As mentioned in the preceding chapter, the unit was in its infancy and this being the first unit in India, producing different types of heavy electrical equipments under one roof, notwithstanding the bottlenecks in supply of raw materials, the amount of loss incurred by the Bhopal unit till the year 1973 was not very alarming.

In order to evaluate the financial performance, ten year data on different economic indicators of BHEL comprising all its units including the one at Bhopal have been presented in Table 3.1. To compare and judge the performance and financial viability of the BHEL Company with others in the public sector, similar data for the ten year period (beginning with the year 1971-72 up to 1980-81) have been presented for all public enterprises in Table 3.2.

BHEL is a capital intensive industry as it produces heavy electrical equipments only. An average public sector enterprise is comparatively less capital intensive. However, if we look through the capital structure of BHEL, it can be seen (Table 3.1) that the rate of increase in capital employed is significantly lower than that of the value of production during the seventies except in the year 1979-80. In the case of all public sector enterprises (Table 3.2), the difference between the two rates is not that significant and in the years 1975-76 and 1978-79 output grew at a slower rate than the capital. The output in BHEL grew at a much faster pace than the public sector undertakings until the late seventies. Thus, in terms of production targets the BHEL seems to have done fairly well as compared to other undertakings within the public sector. However, when we consider indicators like value of production to capital employed, it is favourable in the case of all public sector enterprises compared to BHEL because the latter is a capital intensive unit, which can be seen from the high value of capital employed per employee. Despite this limitation in the beginning of the production process, BHEL has been able to overcome the problem to some extent as this ratio has become less adverse over the years. Similarly, while comparing indicators like (i) material cost to cost of production and (ii) manpower cost to cost of production, one notes that these are higher in the case of BHEL than the public sector enterprises as a whole because the former employs precious imported raw materials. Also, the personnel employed by the BHEL, being

TABLE 3.1 : **Economic indicators of BHEL corporate sector, 1971-72 to 1980-81**

Sl. no.	Indicators	1971-72	1972-73	1973-74	1974-75	1975-76	1976-77	1977-78	1978-79	1979-80	1980-81
1.	Capital employed (Rs. in lakh)	23,940	26,157	33,259	44,494	49,936	40,413	41,668	48,517	63,228	68,979
2.	% increase in capital employed	—	9.26	27.15	33.78	12.23	—19.07	3.10	16.44	30.32	9.10
3.	Value of production (Rs. in lakh)	10,314	14,140	23,094	31,108	42,140	47,097	55,392	65,910	72,889	80,703
4.	% increase in value of production	—	37.09	63.32	34.70	35.46	11.76	17.61	18.99	10.59	10.72
5.	Value of production to capital employed	43.08	54.06	69.44	69 91	84.39	116.54	132.94	135.85	115.28	117.00
6.	Material cost to cost of production	52.02	56.74	61.56	56.68	60.97	59.09	55.19	55.38	56.75	56.56
7.	Manpower cost to cost of production	19.00	18.75	16.60	19.95	16.12	15.00	14.61	13.38	13.49	13.62
8.	Value added to capital employed	22.45	27.69	34.69	39.60	43.10	61.80	68.50	71.50	53.70	40.10
9.	Average capital per employee (Rs.)	65,769	64,268	74,239	93,279	96,031	75397	74,274	80,997	1,00,362	1,01,440
10.	Average monthly emoluments per employee (Rs.)	449	504	642	931	965	975	1107	1177	1277	1401

11. Value of production per man month (Rs.)	23,61	28,95	42,96	54,35	67,53	73,22	82,28	91,69	96,41	98,90
12. Gross profit to capital employed	5.62	9.82	11.95	15.95	17.71	22.84	19.53	16.28	12.66	11.73
13. Profit before tax to net worth	3.43	19.87	28.62	36.83	33.25	33.82	28.09	22.73	17.50	13.57
14. Net profit to paid up capital	3.01	11.31	20.77	32.71	19.26	21.63	19.63	19.35	26.21	17.76

Source : ***Annual Report on the Working of Industrial and Commercial Undertakings of the Central Government*** **(Public Enterprise Survey) Vol I & III, from 1971 to 1981, Ministry of Finance, Bureau of Public Enterprises, New Delhi.**

TABLE 3.2 : **Economic indicators of all public sector concerns, 1971-72 to 1980-81**

Sl. No.	Indicators	1971-72	1972-73	1973-74	1974-75	1975-76	1976-77	1977-78	1978-79	1979-80	1980-81
1.	Capital employed (Rs. in lakh)	4,01,780	4,75,600	5,25,590	6,62,715	8,82,430	10,86,141	12,13,020	13,96,908	16,18,234	18,23,076
2.	% increase in capital employed	—	18.37	10.51	26.09	33.15	23.08	11.68	15.16	15.84	12.66
3.	Value of production (Rs. in lakh)	3,97,200	5,26,202	6,77,669	10,21,719	11,68,841	14,54,223	18,02,548	19,06,096	23,28,992	28,64,532
4.	% increase in value of production	—	32.48	28.78	50.77	14.40	24.42	23.95	5.74	22.19	22.99
5.	Value of production to capital employed	98.9	110.6	128.9	154.2	132.4	133.9	148.6	136.5	143.9	157.1
6.	Material cost to cost of production	—	16.3	18.5	23.0	22.7	23.2	—	24.2	25.7	29.3
7.	Manpower cost to cost of production	—	9.4	10.9	10.2	9.9	9.1	—	9.7	8.9	9.6
8.	Value added to capital employed*	—	—	45.97	48.35	48.68	34.62	—	37.15	36.52	36.14
9.	Average capital per employee (Rs.)	57,292	51,017	39,095	46,285	58,640	68,958	—	82,026	91,168	99,180
10.	Average monthly emoluments per employee (Rs.)	493	484	464	617	748	745	837	933	1,039	1,184

11. Value of production per man month (Rs.)	4,720	4,704	4,201	5,946	6,473	7,694	9,170	9,327	10,934	12,875
12. Gross profit to capital employed	4.2	5.1	6.3	8.4	7.6	9.4	7.5	7.7	7.6	7.8
13. Profit before tax to net worth	7.4	6.3	7.1	8.3	6.8	8.8	—	3.1	3.1	0.5
14. Net profit to paid up capital	—0.7	3.5	1.9	4.9	2.9	4.7	—	—0.6	—0.9	—2.1

* N.B.—Only for Enterprises producing and selling goods.

Source : *Annual Report on the Working of Industrial and Commercial Undertakings of the Central Government*(Public Enterprise Survey) Vol. I & III from 1971 to 1981, Ministry of Finance, Bureau of Public Enterprises, New Delhi.

highly technical, start on a higher salary than their counterparts in other units. We can see from the tables that the monthly emoluments per employee in regard to BHEL is quite high compared to the average monthly emoluments of all public sector units. Furthermore, BHEL being one of the unit of heavy electrical equipment, its increase in the rate of production depends upon the demand for its products. That is why the rate of increase in the value of production has gone down occasionally compared to a few other public sector enterprises, especially in recent years. But if we take the indicators like value added to capital employed, it works out to be fairly high in the case of BHEL except in the last two years, despite the rise in the price of the raw materials. For other public undertakings this, indicator is fluctuating and often works out to be less than that of BHEL. This is an indication of higher productivity of the BHEL workers than that of any average public sector undertaking.

The performance and financial viability of public sector or private sector may also be judged by taking into account its profit structure. Despite its relatively low value of production per unit of capital and per man month, coupled with high percentage of manpower and material costs to total cost of production than the public enterprises as a whole, BHEL has maintained its profitability throughout the years under consideration and now it has become one among the top ten profit earning public sector units in India. If we go through the last three indicators in Tables 3.1 and 3.2, it can be seen that the percentages of gross profit to capital employed, profit before tax to net worth and net profit to paid up capital have always remained high in the case of BHEL as compared to the public sector enterprises as a whole. In fact, the ratio of net profit to paid up capital in the case of public enterprises as a whole is either negative or positive only at the margin in all the ten years under consideration.

The financial performance of the BHEL is comparable with that of the private sector enterprises that operate solely with profit motives, except in the year 1971-72. This clearly indicates the success of the BHEL in terms of commercial profitability. Of course, one may say that BHEL is having monopoly power over its products, and consequently can charge high prices to earn the desired rate of profit. But the pricing policy of BHEL is regulated by the Government. According to these regulations and the prevailing practices, the prices have to be less than the landed cost of similar products in the country.

Besides, the BHEL has made substantial indirect contributions to Government exchequer since its inception in terms of excise duty, customs duty, sales tax, interest on government loans, income tax, dividend, etc. Up to the year ending 31st March 1981, BHEL had contributed a total revenue of Rs. 1,24,499 lakh into the Government treasury—Rs. 62,309 lakh as customs duty, Rs. 12,597 lakh as sales tax, Rs. 14,038 lakh as excise duty, Rs. 18,665 lakh as interest on government loans, Rs. 12,870 lakh as income tax and Rs. 4,020 lakh as dividends. Out of this, the BHEL unit of Bhopal has contributed a total sum of Rs. 23,983 lakh since its inception—Rs. 6,557 lakh as interest on Government loans, Rs. 4,182 lakh as excise duty, Rs. 16,218 lakh as custom duty, Rs. 3,582 lakh as sales tax. The contribution of the Bhopal unit constitutes 19.26 per cent of the total BHEL's contribution to the national exchequer. This clearly shows that BHEL, Bhopal has made a significant contribution towards the Government revenues. Judging from all these perspectives, we can say that the BHEL has not only played an important role in providing one of the major inputs for the development of the power sector but has been, at the same time, a profit earning sector. It has been able to generate some amount of investible surplus not only for its own expansion and growth but also for the industrial growth of the country.

4

BHEL IN THE INDUSTRIAL GROWTH OF BHOPAL REGION

THE reorganisation of Indian States resulted in Bhopal becoming the State capital of Madhya Pradesh in 1956. Before Independence, it was a feudal state ruled by the Nawabs. Because of its feudal structure and associated socio-political constraints, the economy of Bhopal was in a very backward state. It had more than 80 per cent of its population, directly deriving their livelihood from agriculture which was itself in its primitive stage. The process of industrial growth that could provide increasing employment to the people in the secondary sector was almost absent. There were only two medium units like the New Bhopal Textile Mills and M/s Straw Products established in 1938 and 1939, respectively.

It is assumed that when a key industry like the BHEL unit is established in a backward region it would help in the growth of other industries in the region, through backward and forward linkages and infrastructural development. In the present chapter, an attempt has been made to evaluate the impact of the BHEL unit on the pattern of industrial growth in the Bhopal region since the setting up of the unit.

Patterns of industrial growth in Bhopal

In Chapter 2, it is stated that production in BHEL started in July 1960 and since then the unit has grown into a big public sector undertaking over the years and is currently providing direct employment to about 19,000 people. Besides, the unit has helped in setting up of very many large, medium and small-scale units in Bhopal city and its hinterland through its linkages and infrastructural support. According to the data supplied by the Sub-contracting Division of the BHEL, it makes purchases of inputs from about 166 industrial units in Bhopal including 48 BHEL ancillaries. In the year ending in December, 1982 (beginning from the financial year April, 1982), all these units supplied goods worth Rs. 9 crore. To develop and sustain these units, BHEL extends help in the form of expertise, tooling technology, use of new materials, testing, inspection services etc.

In order to assess the role played by the BHEL unit in the industrial growth of Bhopal region and to determine the extent to which its growth rate and growth pattern are different from those of the State, an analysis of the patterns of industrial growth in Bhopal city has been attempted on the basis of the data from the Establishment Tables of 1961 and 1971 Censuses (Appendices 4.1 to 4.6). We have chosen these two points of time for the analysis since production in the BHEL unit started only in July 1960 whereas Bhopal was made the state capital in 1956. Consequently, we can say that whatever industrial growth took place during the decade 1951-61 was due to the setting up of the state capital and construction of BHEL unit in Bhopal. However, the pattern of industrial growth together with the changes in the industrial structure during the decade 1961-71 can be explained largely in terms of the direct or indirect impact of the BHEL unit alone. The analysis would have been more precise and up to date had we been able to get the economic data from the 1981 Census. This has not been possible as the Establishment and Economic Tables are yet to be published for most of the states. From Appendix 4.2, it can be seen that Bhopal city had a high concentration of units belonging to the following major groups of Manufacturing and Repair divisions in 1971. They are : (1) food products ; (2) beverage, tobacco and tobacco products ; (3) textile products including wearing apparel other than footwear ; (4) leather and fur products (5) rubber, plastic, petroleum and coal products ; (6) chemicals and chemical products ; (7) basic metal and alloy industries ; (8) machinery and machine tools and parts except electrical machinery ; (9) electrical machinery, apparatus, appliances and parts ; (10) transport equipments and parts and (11) repairs. As a matter of fact, of the 19 broad categories of the Census classification, these 11 major groups had a larger percentage of total units in Bhopal in 1971 compared to the figures for the State or the district.

It should be noted that the concentration of units belonging to the following five categories in Bhopal city, as measured through the location quotients, are extremely high : (i) basic metal and alloy industries ; (ii) manufacture of machinery, machine tools and parts except electrical machinery ; (iii) manufacture of electrical machinery apparatus, appliances and parts and (v) repairs. These five broad categories seem to have developed in Bhopal due to the existence of BHEL unit as they have direct and indirect linkages with Heavy Electrical Equipment Plant. It may be seen in Appendix 4.3 that out of 19 broad categories in the manufacturing division, four major groups of industries *viz.*, 33, 35, 37 and 39 have a higher growth rate of units in urban areas of Sehore district compared to the State's growth rate in urban areas during 1961-71. As the share of Bhopal city in the number of units located in Sehore urban areas is more than 80 per cent, we can say emphatically that these units grew in Bhopal city because of their linkages with the BHEL unit. Of course, one may question, why there was a negative growth for the units in the major group-36, i.e. *manufacture of electrical machinery and appliance etc.*, in the urban areas of Sehore district during sixties. It is noted from the Establishment Tables of 1961 and 1971 Censuses that the unit like BHEL was not included in the major group-36 due to some reason. But still the fall in the number of smaller units in the major group-36 is conspicuous and so is the fall in the number of bigger units in Sehore district and M.P. It seems that a few big units in the State as well as in the district, manufacturing electrical machinery, closed down their sub-units, as they were priced out of the market due to the superior quality and low price of the BHEL products. It may be noted that the units belonging to the major group-36 were concentrated in Bhopal and the non-household manufacturing units in this group claimed a major share of all industrial units in Bhopal city as well as in Sehore district. It can also be seen in Appendix 4.4 that for the major group *viz.*, manufacturing of electrical machinery and other electrical items in non-household industrial sector, Madhya Pradesh had only a share of 0.98 per cent in the total units in India whereas Sehore district had a share of 21.54 per cent units in M.P. and Bhopal had a share of 42.86 per cent of units in

Sehore district in 1971. It seems, the units which were supplying complementary inputs and parts to BHEL grew significantly—the aspect which would be covered at a later stage in the present chapter.

One may question as to whether it is possible to explain the growth of industries and changes in the industrial structure in Bhopal region in terms of the location of the BHEL unit (see Fig. 4.1). Bhopal was made the state capital of Madhya Pradesh in 1956, as mentioned above, and being the capital city it might have attracted entrepreneurs to establish industrial units. On account of high infrastructural development, the steps taken by the State government to establish industrial estates in Bhopal and the provision of other benefits to the industrialists, a number of manufacturing units could have come to the city and its hinterland during the period under investigation. From the types of non-household manufacturing units concentrated in Bhopal city and Sehore district, we can examine whether the location of a large number of these units can be explained in terms of the BHEL or the other factors mentioned above.

According to 1971 Census, the population of Madhya Pradesh was 7.60 per cent of the country's population whereas the State had a share of 4.11 per cent of units and 3.86 per cent of employment in the non-household manufacturing industry in India. This clearly shows that M.P. is an industrially backward state. Sehore district, on the other hand, had a 2.60 per cent of M.P.'s population in 1971 and its shares in total units and employment in non-household manufacturing sector were 5.35 per cent and 5.57 per cent, respectively. This clearly indicates that Sehore district is relatively advanced industrially in the State. The city of Bhopal had a share of 70.60 per cent of the units and 44.95 per cent of the total employment in non-household manufacturing sector, although it had a population share of 35.47 per cent in Sehore district in 1971.

Due to the changes in the definition of workers in the 1971 Census, the categories of workers in 1961 and 1971 are simply not comparable and as such the percentages of workers in 1971 to total population for India and Madhya Pradesh were significantly below the corresponding figures in 1961 (Table 4.1). But still we can see that the percentage increase of workers in manufacturing industries during 1961-71 was significant both in

TABLE 4.1 : Occupational pattern in India, Madhya Pradesh, Sehore district, Huzur tahsil and Bhopal city, 1961 and 1971

Name of Place	% of workers to total population			% of workers in primary sector		% of workers in secondary sector		% of workers in tertiary sector		% in Manufacturing industries	
	1961	1971	1981	1961	1971	1961	1971	1961	1971	1961	1971
India	42.98	32.92	33.44	72.20	72.56	11.40	10.69	16.02	16.74	10.61	9.46
Madhya Pradesh	52.30	36.72	33.49	82.22	81.75	7.98	7.47	9.80	10.78	6.96	6.68
Sehore district	46.29	32.76	35.10	64.08	59.57	15.57	14.44	20.36	26.00	11.08	12.58
Huzur tahsil	40.05	29.81	...	26.63	21.20	33.40	27.18	39.97	51.61	21.17	23.50
Bhopal city	36.91	28.66	28.64	3.78	3.23	43.98	32.83	52.23	63.94	27.22	28.47

Source : Census of India, 1961 and 1971, Part II (A), *General Population Tables*, Madhya Pradesh.

Sehore district and Huzur tahsil, wherein Bhopal city is located. The non-household industrial workers in Sehore district, Huzur tahsil and Bhopal city increased at about three per cent during the decade 1961-71 while the corresponding growth rate for India and M.P. was one per cent only. Thus, we can say that the growth rate of industrial employment in Bhopal, which is significantly above that of the State, is primarily due to the rapid industrialisation that occurred after the establishment of the BHEL unit.

In order to make our argument more convincing, we may take the help of Appendix 4.5. It is seen that there was a structural change in the process of industrialization in M.P., Sehore district as well as Bhopal city during the decade 1961-71, with the share of rural areas in the total industrial units going down significantly in the district and the State. It is important that the proportion of the units with 10 and more workers to total units had gone up during 1961-71 in both urban and rural areas of Sehore district. However, the growth in these units in the State of Madhya Pradesh was higher than Sehore district.

The major groups 20-21 to 39 falling in the Manufacturing and Repair Division 2-3 can be classified into three broad categories :

(i) Consumer goods industries comprising major groups 20-21 to 29 ;
(ii) Chemical goods industries consisting of major groups 30, 31 and 32 ; and,
(iii) Engineering goods industries comprising major groups 33 to 39.

It can be seen from Appendix 4.5. that the units with 10 or more persons in both rural and urban areas as well as units with 1-9 workers along with the units with unspecified number of workers increased at a very fast rate in the case of consumer goods industries, chemicals good industries and engineering goods industries in M.P. during 1961-71. This, however, is not the case in the rural and urban areas of Sehore district. While there was a substantial increase in the units with 10 and more persons in the case of engineering and chemical goods in the district, there was a fall of units with 1-9 persons (plus units with unspecified number of workers) in the same categories. Side by side, we can see that there was a decline in the share of units with 10 or more persons in the consumer goods sector in the urban areas of Sehore district although it remained generally invariant in the case of rural areas. It may also be noted that Bhopal had a major share in both chemical and engineering goods industries in 1971. In fact, these two groups of industries had direct linkages with the BHEL unit. Thus, it would appear that the BHEL unit in Bhopal has been able to bring about considerable change in the structure of the manufacturing activities in both Bhopal city and Sehore district. Also, it has helped the growth of small and medium size units in the organized sector in Bhopal and Sehore district within a decade of its existence, whereas the number of informal units in the case of engineering and chemicals goods industries, has declined considerably.

Again, it can be seen from Appendix 4.6 that engineering goods industries in Sehore district and Bhopal city had a larger share in the total manufacturing units compared to the State in 1971. In the case of Sehore district and Bhopal city, the share of consumer goods industries in all manufacturing and repairing units (division 2-3) was 70.43 per cent and 58.13 per cent respectively whereas in the case of M.P., it was 72 per cent. On the other hand, the share of engineering units and their share in total employment were 17.97 per cent and 18.63 per cent in M P., 20.75 per cent and 39.62 per cent in Sehore district and 38.13 per cent and 31.08 per cent in Bhopal city, respectively. This clearly shows that Bhopal city has a larger base of engineering goods industries, which can be attributed primarily to the location of the BHEL unit.

In order to back up the conclusion obtained from the secondary data, a survey of about 50 industrial units, both connected and unconnected with the BHEL factory was attempted through a questionnaire. Of these units, about 16 units were ancillary to BHEL, Bhopal. The sample units belonged to different industrial categories like engineering, electrical and electronic, chemicals such as pesticides, soap, dry battery cell, etc. ; wood and wood products and the miscellaneous units like cotton textiles, p inting and publishing industries, flour mills and so on. For the sake of convenience, these sam le units are broadly classified into five categories, *viz.* (i) engineering and machinery

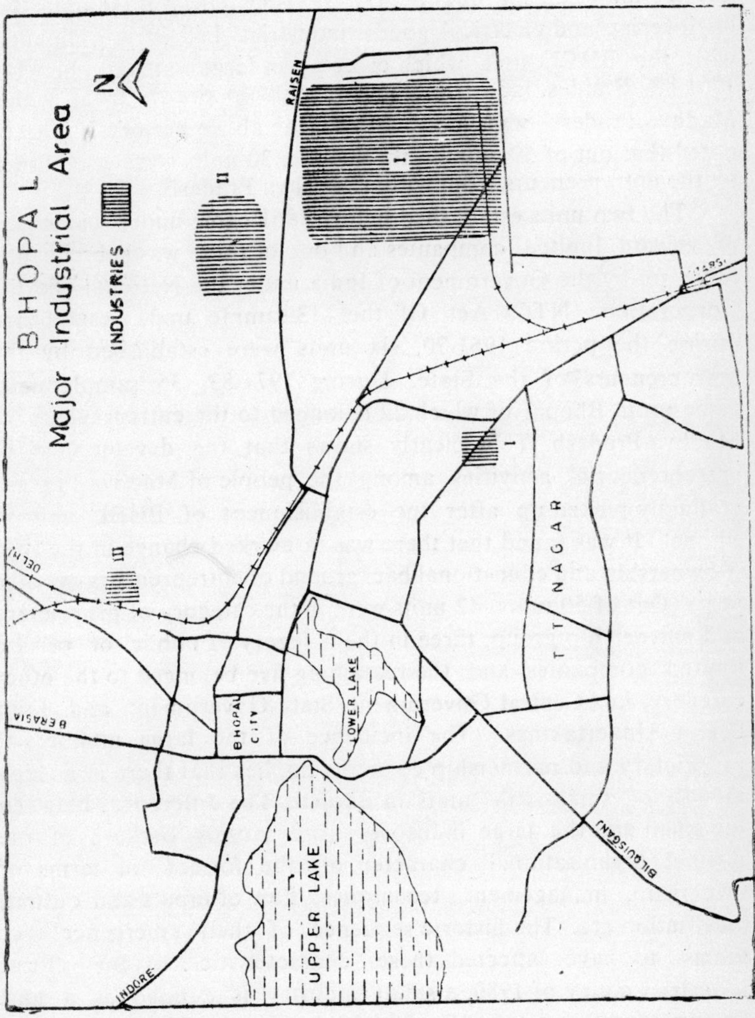
BHOPAL
Major Industrial Area
INDUSTRIES
N
I
II
III
RAISEN
DELHI
BERASIA
INDORE
BHOPAL CITY
LOWER LAKE
UPPER LAKE
T T NAGAR
BILQUISGANJ

FIG. 4.1

units, (ii) electrical units, (iii) wood and wood products units, (iv) chemical units and (v) miscellaneous units (Appendix 4.7).

It is seen in the appendix that there were only two units established prior to 1961 whereas 13 units came up during 1961-70 and 35 units during the period 1971-83. Of all these units, the engineering and electrical goods industries had strong linkages with the BHEL unit which came up in large numbers between 1961-83. Besides, industrial entrepreneurship drawn from within Madhya Pradesh was more during the above period. It is to be noted that out of 50 units in the sample, 30 units were established by the entrepreneurs from within Madhya Pradesh.

The two units established before 1961 came under categories of private limited companies and one of these was subsequently taken up by the Government of India under the National Textile Corporation (NTC) Act. Of the 13 sample units established during the period 1961-70, six units were established by the entrepreneurs of the State. During 1971-83, 35 sample units came up in Bhopal of which 22 belonged to the entrepreneurs of Madhya Pradesh. This clearly shows that the development of entrepreneurial activities among the people of Madhya Pradesh gradually picked up after the establishment of BHEL unit in Bhopal. It was found that there was a marked change in the type of ownership and educational background of entrepreneurs over the years. Out of 50 units, 42 units were in the category of proprietary and partnership group, three in the category of public or private limited companies and the remaining five belonged to the other category, i.e. Central Government, State Government and Joint Sector Undertakings. The incidence of the large number of proprietary and partnership concerns implies that there is a high growth of small-scale units in Bhopal. The differences between the small and the large industries arise largely because of the distinct organisational character of the former in terms of ownership, management, techniques, flow of inputs and output, localisation etc. The historic sequence of their emergence too, seems to have affected these characteristics. In the official industrial policy of 1980, a small industry is defined as a unit having investment upto Rs. 20 lakh in plant and machinery. In the case of ancillary unit, the limit has been put at Rs. 25 lakh and a "tiny unit" as one with investment up to Rs. 2 lakh.

There has been a fast growth of entrepreneurship from

among the technically qualified personnel in the State. Out of 50 units in the sample, 34 units were established by the people holding technical degrees or diplomas and the remaining 16 units were established by the entrepreneurs having general degrees or ordinary educational qualifications. Moreover, it was found that most of the entrepreneurs did not have much experience at the t.me of the establishment of their units in Bhopal and there were very few entrepreneurs among the sampled units who had either business or industrial links earlier. This implies that the industrial growth taking place in Bhopal in recent years is primarily in the hands of modern, non-business community and not the traditional business class. It is to be noted that besides extending patronage to the small scale units in Bhopal, the BHEL unit has encouraged its own employees to establish ancillary units. In the sample, there are four ex-BHEL employees who have established ancillary units.

It is seen from Appendix 4.7 that 4,637 workers are employed by these sample units. Of this, about 34.62 per cent are skilled workers and the rest belong to the semi-skilled and unskilled categories. Again, among the skilled workers, 44.60 per cent are employed by the engineering and electrical goods industries only. Since most of these units recruit labour from local sources and they provide in-plant training to their workers and also often promote unskilled and semi-skilled workers to the skilled category, it can be said that these units have helped the process of skill formation. Besides, compared to the earnings of unskilled and skilled workers in informal sectors in Bhopal ranging from Rs. 10 to 15 and Rs. 15 to 30 respectively, an unskilled worker employed in these sample unit earns from Rs. 7 to 15 in unskilled or semi-skilled category and from Rs. 15 to 40 in skilled category. Since very few units are seasonal in nature, the process of industrialization in Bhopal has prov ded a permanent source of income to the industrial workforce. These units, besides providing direct employment to workers in the industrial sector, have helped in the expansion of the service sector in Bhopal as may be seen in Table 4.1 compiled from the data of 1961, 1971 and 1981 Censuses.

In our sample study of 50 units, about 17 units purchase their raw materials through organised agencies like Madhya Pradesh Laghu Udyog Nigam (MPLUN), BHEL, Steel Authori of India Limited (SAIL), Minerals and Metal Trading Corporation, Food Corporation of India and others. Quite a few of them purchase raw materials from MPLUN and BHEL in Bhopal. Besides, about 22 units make their purchases from outside markets of Bombay, Delhi, Calcutta, Madras, Indore etc. It is to be noted that most of the units, especially those producing engineering and electrical goods, either purchase a portion of their inputs from BHEL or do some jobworks through the materials supplied by BHEL.

It is important to note that our sample units sell 18.17 per cent of their total output to BHEL only. The units in engineering and electrical goods category sell 49.41 per cent and 43.34 per cent respectively, of their total output to BHEL. Thus, we can say that BHEL has directly helped in the growth and capital formation of about 50 per cent of engineering and electrical goods industries in Bhopal. The corresponding percentage for wood and wood product industries works out as 70.67 which seems to be rather high. This may be due to the selection of fewer units in this category in our sample and also due to the inclusion of one ancillary unit of the BHEL which sells its total output to the latter. However, on the whole, we can say that the BHEL is directly responsible for the growth of about 20 per cent of industrial units including their capital formation and employment generation in Bhopal since its inception in 1960.

We would have got a better picture of the linkage effect of the BHEL in Bhopal had we been successful in getting data on industrial establishments from secondary sources till the year 1981. Also, we could not estimate the figures on changes in the sectoral composition of income in Bhopal city and the contribution of engineering and electrical goods industries in the secondary sector. The information from the Directorate of Industries and Directorate of Economics and Statistics, Madhya Pradesh was inadequate for the purpose. However, we could compile data to bring out the growth and the structure of these industries in Bhopal district, as may be seen in Table 4.2.

Besides these small scale units, 14 large and medium industries including one in public sector and another in joint sector (excluding BHEL), were in operation in Bhopal district in the year 1977 (Table 4.3). There has not been much addition to the la ge and medium scale industrial units in the late seventies.

TABLE 4.2 : **Small-scale industrial units, investment and employment in Bhopal district till 31st March 1980**

Type of industry	No.	Investment (Rs. in lakh)	Employment
Agriculture based industries	39	23.80	292
Forest based industries	630	48.50	1,043
Mineral based industries	90	30.34	865
Animal goods industries	46	1.40	175
Engineering goods industries	354	182.93	717
Electrical and electronic goods industries	40	27.07	413
Chemical goods industries	93	13.35	191
Demand based industries	182	111.70	1,020
Repairs and others	225	85.25	1,590
Total	1699	524.33	6,310

Source : *Four Year Action Plan 1979-83*, pp. 25-66 ; District Industries Centre, Bhopal

TABLE 4.3 : **Large and medium industries in Bhopal district in 1977**

Type of industry	No.	Investment (Rs in lakh)	Employment
Engineering goods industries	4	302	711
Electrical and electronics goods industries	2	254	421
Chemical goods industries	4	125	588*
Miscellaneous units	4	313	2,490
Total	14	994	4,210

*This excludes employment figure of Union Carbide Industries Ltd., Bhopal.

Source : *Industrial Statistics 1977*, Directorate of Industries, Madhya Pradesh.

Thus, we can say that there were over 1,700 non-household manufacturing units in 1980 with a capital investment of Rs. 1,500 lakh, employing about 11,000 people excluding BHEL, in the district of Bhopal. Out of this, 400 units were engineering and electrical goods industries with a capital investment of Rs. 766 lakh and employment capacity of about 2,260. As it has been said earlier, BHEL makes purchases from about 166 industrial units in Bhopal, most of them being engineering and electrical goods industries. So we can safely say that the BHEL unit in Bhopal is directly linked with the development of about 40 per cent of engineering/electrical goods industries.

Apart from that, BHEL has made indirect contribution in the process of industrial growth in Bhopal. BHEL, Bhopal has about 19,000 employees working in different divisions and its township has approximately one lakh population at present. Since BHEL employees are well paid, drawing a monthly average salary of above Rs. 1,200, the per capita expenditure of the people in BHEL township would be higher than that of others in Bhopal city or in the country as a whole. Even if we assume somewhat lower average per capita expenditure for the people in the BHEL township, say at Rs. 1,800 annually, they must be consuming goods worth Rs. 18 crore every year including the consumer durables. A significant sum of this must be spent on the consumer goods including chemical goods. So we can say that the high rate of growth of consumer goods and chemical industries since 1961 is partly due to the BHEL which has generated substantial demand for their goods through the employees and their dependants.

To sum up, BHEL, Bhopal has played a significant role in determining the pace and pattern of industrial growth in the Bhopal region. Notwithstanding its basic objective of producing power equipments for the country as a whole, it has helped the growth of a large number of engineering and electrical goods industries through its patronisation and ancillarisation programmes, unlike several other public sector heavy industries. As a result, it has been able to come up as one among the best ten public sector manufacturing industries with excellent performance results in recent years. The medium and small-scale units supported by BHEL, including the ancillaries, help in minimizing the cost of production and maximizing capacity utilization by supplying inputs and finished jobworks to the BHEL, as the former have lower cost of labour and better capacity utilization.

5

CHANGING STRUCTURE OF BHOPAL CITY

Geographical Setting

BHOPAL city is one of the rare examples of man-made cities that are surrounded by small hills and lakes on all sides. Because of the existence of planned township like BHEL and the co-existence of planned localities like Tantya Tope Nagar, New Market, Arera Colony, Habibganj and Jawahar Chowk along with old localities like Jahangirabad and Ibrahimpura, Bhopal city like Delhi appears divided into two parts, *viz.* New and Old areas. The city is situated at a height of about 600 metre above the sea level and connected by rails and roads to all important parts of the country. It has developed into an important industrial and trading centre of India over the years especially after the establishment of BHEL. Since 1954-55, its hinterland has expanded at a rapid pace and several of the nearby villages have been brought under the municipal boundary from time to time, so that the expanding city population could be provided with housing facilities and other social amenities like parks, play grounds, schools and community halls. A high rate of population growth in the city i.e. from 102,333 in 1951 to 642,329 in 1981, has expanded the geographical area of Bhopal city, considerably.

Historical background

The name of Bhopal city is said to be derived from *Bhojpal* or *Bhojas dam* referring to Raja Bhoja of Dhar, one of whose ministers is said to have built the great dam. But according to Dr. Fleet, the name Bhopal was derived from *Bhupala*, the king. The present city of Bhopal stands on the site of an old town founded by Raja Bhoja of Dhar. The foundation of modern

Bhopal was laid down by Dost Mohammed, the founder of the Bhopal Kingdom. In 1722 he built the Fatehgarh Fort and walls of the present city. The capital of erstwhile Bhopal state was shifted permanently to Bhopal during the reign of Nawab Faiz Ahmed. In 1795, the lower lake Pukhtapur was constructed. During 1808-19 the city population began to sprawl out of the town walls and several new *mohallas* came into existence.

During the years 1819-37, the expansion continued and the Gohar Mahal Palace was constructed. The magnificient mosque Jama-Masjid was constructed in 1856 and a water works was built at the cost of Rs. 5 lakh in 1869. The rapid growth continued in the subsequent decades and in 1884, the Central Railway line (formerly known as Great Indian Peninsular Railway) was laid followed by Ujjain-Bhopal link on the Western Railway in 1885. With this, the trading and commercial activities of the city began to expand. The Hamidia Hospital (then known as Prince of Wales Hospital) was constructed in 1892. In 1910, Ahmedabad Palace was built along with New Idgah and the area on the Shamla Hill was developed. During the Second World War, Bairagarh township began to grow as it was selected for the camping of war prisoners and after the war was over it was merged with the State. Later, the refugees who came into the city due to the partition of the country in 1947 were settled here.

In fact, the turning point in the life of Bhopal city came in November, 1956 when the capital of the newly organised State of Madhya Pradesh was established. Prior to that, the Government of India had taken a decision to set up its first Heavy Electrical Plant in Bhopal. As a result of these, the city of Bhopal saw a large number of migrants coming into the city and settling in its Govindpura, Habibganj and Berkheda localities. Side-by-side, the construction of residential complex at Tantya Tope Nagar, in the south of the old city, the New Secretariat Building, i.e. Vallabh Bhawan, on the top of Arera Hill etc., also took place. With these construction activities, the landscape began to change and a modern city having amenities of urban life came into being during the late fifties.

Changes in the demographic structure of Bhopal city

At the opening of the 20th Century, *i.e.* 1901, the city had returned a population figure of 77,023 and it was not before the next fifty years that it crossed this mark again. The first census of the city took place in 1881. During 1881-91, the population of the city increased by 0.27 per cent. This was followed by an increase of 10 per cent during the next decade *i.e.*, 1891-1901, thus bringing the total population to 77,023. Bhopal was a class-II town in 1901 but its status was reduced to class-III in 1921 due to the sharp decline in population. However, it could become a Class-I town in 1951. Table 5.1 shows the percentage increase in population of Bhopal city from the beginning of the 20th century to the year 1981.

TABLE 5.1 : **Population growth of Bhopal city, 1901-1981**

Year	Population of Bhopal MC	Percent increase in population
1901	77,023	—
1911	56,204	—27.03
1921	45,092	—19.77
1931	60,991	35.26
1941	75.171	23.25
1951	1,02,333	36.13
1961	1,85.374	81.15
1971	3.84,859	107.61
1981	6,72,329	74.69

Source : Census of India, 1971, *District Census Handbook*, Sehore and Census of India, 1981, *Paper 2*, *Provisional Population Totals*.

Note : Population figures are obtained from the respective Censuses, while the growth rates have been computed after making adjustments for the changes in the area of the city.

It may be seen from Table 5.1 that the population growth in Bhopal city has recorded a fantastic increase since 1961, the growth rate during the decades 1961-71 and 1971-81 being 107.61 and 74.69 per cent, respectively. These growth rates were far higher than the country's urban growth rates of 38.20 and 46.02 per cent, respectively. The corresponding growth figures for the State was 46.63 and 56.07 per cent, respectively. This clearly shows the impact of locating the State capital and the BHEL factory on the demographic expansion of Bhopal city.

Apart from that, Bhopal city which accounted for 82.03 per

cent and 85.67 per cent of the total urban population of Sehore district in 1961 and 1971, respectively, had enumerated a maximum percentage of migrants coming from other districts of M.P. coupled with a high percentage of migrants from other states of India as well as foreign countries (Table 5.2). The percentages of people born in other districts of the State to the total population in the years 1961 and 1971 were 17.47 per cent and 18.48 per cent, respectively in the case of Sehore district's urban area, whereas they were 14.03 per cent and 13.51 per cent for the total urban area of Madhya Pradesh. People coming from different states of India claimed a share of 20.17 per cent and 20.14 per cent in 1961 and 1971 for Sehore's Urban areas as compared to the corresponding state (urban) figures of 15.59 per cent and 14.01 per cent. This clearly indicates that the percentage of interstate and interdistrict migrants to Bhopal city had remained very high during the sixties although there was a slight decline in the proportion in the case of M.P. The same tendency has been recorded in the rural areas of the district as well. Thus, we can say that the development since the mid-fifties have given Bhopal a cosmopolitan character.

In order to know whether the heavy migration took place due to the establishment of state capital and the heavy electrical plant at Bhopal or if there were a large number of migrants prior to that, the duration of residence of migrants in Bhopal city has been analysed in Table 5.3. In the total population of 185,374 of the Bhopal M.C. in 1961, about 117,562 (63.42 per cent) were migrants to the city. It is important that 21.06 per cent and 44.81 per cent of these migrants had a stay of less than one year and between 1 and 5 years, respectively. Hence, it can be inferred that a large number of migrants came to Bhopal during 1956-61 that were the years of the establishment of the new capital and the heavy electrical plant at Bhopal. The percentage share of migrants from within the district to the urban areas of Sehore district came down from 5.68 to 3.77 during 1961-71 which suggests that the Bhopal city did not attract migrants from its immediate neighbourhood and the required manpower in the initial stages was drawn from other towns in the State and from outside the State.

Table 5.4 indicates that out of 2,22,948 population in Bhopal town group which included BHEL township and Bairagarh

TABLE 5.2 : **Percentage of migrants in Madhya Pradesh and Sehore district in the years 1961 and 1971**

Category of population	M.P. rural population		M.P. urban population		Sehore district rural population		Sehore district urban population	
	1961	1971	1961	1971	1961	1971	1961	1971
1	2	3	4	5	6	7	8	9
(a) Born in place of enumeration	64.92	67.47	52.67	57.45	64.37	67.62	50.17	53.69
(b) Born elsewhere in the district of enumeration	26.54	24.00	14.19	12.73	23.58	20.04	5.68	3.77
(c) Born in other districts of the state	5.67	5.66	14.03	13.51	10.21	11.31	17.47	18.48
(d) Born in other states	2.73	2.37	15.59	14.01	1.63	0.92	20.17	20.14
1. Andhra Pradesh	0.04	0.04	0.62	0.62	0.02	0.01	0.51	0.56
2. Assam	0.03	0.02	0.02	0.03	—	—	0.03	0.06
3. Bihar	0.13	0.15	0.49	0.65	0.02	0.01	0.36	0.75
4. Gujarat	0.06	0.05	0.68	0.55	0.02	0.03	0.48	0.46
5. Haryana	—	0.02	—	0.23	—	0.02	—	0.37
6. Himachal Pradesh	—	0.001	—	0.08	—	0.002	—	0.10
7. Jammu & Kashmir	0.001	0.001	0.05	0.05	0.003	0.003	0.08	0.06
8. Karnataka	0.002	0.002	0.11	0.10	0.004	—	0.26	0.31
9. Kerala	0.01	0.01	0.34	0.50	0.008	0.02	0.64	1.57
10. Maharashtra	0.49	0.41	3.57	2.91	0.20	0.10	5.91	4.68
11. Orissa	0.34	0.30	0.47	0.53	—	0.003	0.04	0.06
12. Punjab	0.06	0.04	0.06	0.59	0.08	0.02	1.28	0.88

TABLE 5.2 : (*Contd.*)

1	2	3	4	5	6	7	8	9
13. Rajasthan	0.62	0.42	2.36	1.69	0.59	0.33	1.60	1.20
14. Tamil Nadu	0.01	0.01	0.34	0.22	0.03	0.003	0.99	0.91
15 Uttar Pradesh	0.90	0.85	4.92	4.63	0.64	0.36	7.29	7.33
16. West Bengal	0.03	0.04	0.39	0.45	0.005	0.003	0.31	0.39
17. Other States & Union Territories	0.004	0.004	0.17	0.18	0.01	0.005	0.39	0.45
(e) Foreign Ccuntries	0.15	0.50	3.51	2.28	0.20	0.12	6.60	3.82

Source : 1. Census of India, 1961 *Migration Tables* Part IIC (ii-A), Vol, 8, Madhya Pradesh.
2. Census of India, 1971. *Migration Tables* Part IID (Vol. 1), Series 10, Madhya Pradesh.

TABLE 5.3 : **Percentage of migrants in Bhopal city according to their period of stay, 1961**

Total Migra nts	Less than one year	1—5 years	6—10 years	11—15 years	16+ years	Period not stated
100	21.06	44.81	10.84	12.89	7.22	3.17

Source : Census of India. 1961 *District Census Handbook* Sehore pp. XIV.

TABLE 5.4 : **Birth place of population in Bhopal town group, 1961**

Sl. No.	Name of place	Population	Percentage to total population
1.	Total population in Bhopal town group	2,22,948	100
2.	Born in India	2,05,912	92.36
3.	Born in M.P.	1,54,386	69.22
4.	Born in place of enumeration	1,05,386	47.27
5.	Born elsewhere in the district	8,244	3.70
6.	Other districts of M.P.	40,685	18.25
	(i) Contiguous Districts	14,829	6.65
	(a) Indore	3,120	1.40
	(b) Dewas	357	0.16
	(c) Raisen	2,364	1.06
	(d) Vidisha	2,564	1.15
	(e) Rajgarh	781	0.35
	(f) Guna	1,086	0.49
	(g) Shajapur	477	0.21
	(h) Hoshangabad	4,086	1.83
	(ii) Other Districts of M.P.	25,856	11.60
7.	Born in Other States	51,597	23.14
	(a) Andhra Pradesh	—	0.60
	(b) Maharashtra	—	7.03
	(c) Uttar Pradesh	—	8.08
	(d) Rajasthan	—	1.77
	(e) Kerala	—	0.76
	(f) Tamil Nadu	—	1.20
	(g) Punjab	—	1.44
	(h) Bihar	—	0.43
	(i) Orissa	—	0.05
	(j) Assam	—	0.04
	(k) Gujarat		0.52
	(l) Jammu & Kashmir	—	0.09
	(m) Karnataka	—	0.32
	(n) West Bengal	—	0.37
	(o) Others	—	0.44
8.	Born Outside India	—	7.62
	(a) Asia	—	7.60
	(b) Europe	—	0.02

Source : Census of India, 1961 *District Census Handbook* Sehore, pp. XIII.

locality in the year 1961, about 23.14 per cent and 7.62 per cent of the population were born in other states of India and in foreign countries, respectively. In addition, 6.65 per cent of the population were born in the contiguous districts of Bhopal and 11.60 per cent in other districts of the State. From these tables, however, it is not clear whether the large scale migration was due to the establishment of heavy electrical plant or to the shifting of state capital to Bhopal.

Apart from the changes in the population composition since 1961 in Bhopal city, it is seen from Appendix 5.1 that the percentage of workers in the age-group of 15-59 was higher in Bhopal city during the years 1961 and 1971, compared to the urban areas of Madhya Pradesh and Sehore district. Also, the number of child workers in the age-group of 0-14 were comparatively less in Bhopal city than in the case of M.P. and Sehore urban areas. A similar observation can be made in the case of the people in the old-age as well. The percentage of population in the age-group of 60 and above in the Bhopal city in 1971 was lower than in M.P. or Sehore (urban). Bhopal city had a higher percentage of workers in the age-group of 15-59 and lower percentage of child workers and old-age workers largely due to the incidence of employment in the public sector and other organised enterprises. The percentage of people above sixty increased in the year 1971 which may be due to increased longevity of its population because of the over all socio-economic prosperity.

Changes in the linguistic composition of population

In 1951 Census, Sehore district had returned 38 languages, including dialects of Hindi and Rajasthani, as mother-tongues of its population. But in 1961 Census, it recorded as many as 73 languages as mother tongues. Table 5.5 presents percentage increase or decrease in different major linguistic groups in Sehore district. Since Bhopal city has a major share in the population of the district, the unusual increase in the population speaking different languages during the decade 1951-61 reflects the pattern of migration into Bhopal city due to the establishment of the heavy electrical plant. This fact can be noted in Table 5.6. It is seen that in the major languages (except Hindi) spoken by the people in Sehore district in 1961, Bhopal town group claims

TABLE 5.5 : **Main languages spoken by people in Sehore district, 1951 and 1961**

Mother Tongue	Persons		Per cent increase or decrease over the decade 1951-61
	1951	1961	
All languages	5,21,116	7,54,684	44.82
Hindi	3,79,743	5,74,290	51.23
Urdu	1,11,905	1,07,592	—3.85
Gujarati	337	3,353	894.96
Gondi	3,878	3,799	—2.04
Bengali	430	1,852	330.70
Malayalam	29	1,765	5,986.21
Marathi	754	15,765	1,990.85
Punjabi	1,561	7,082	353.68
Tamil	55	2,898	5,169.09
Telugu	5	1,710	34,100.00
Sindhi	13,367	23,870	78.57
Marwari	1,353	2,551	88.54

Source : Census of India, 1961 *District Census Handbook*, Sehore.

TABLE 5.6 : **Main languages spoken by the people in Sehore district and Bhopal town group, 1961**

Language	Persons in Sehore district	Persons in Bhopal Town group	Bhopal's share in the district
Bengali	1,852	1,800	97.19
Gujarati	3,353	2,921	87.12
Hindi	5,74,290	88,030	15.33
Malayalam	1,765	1,700	96.32
Marathi	15,765	14,679	93.11
Marwari	2,551	1,014	39.75
Punjabi	7,082	6,600	93.19
Sindhi	23.870	22,377	93.75
Tamil	2,898	2,825	97.48
Telugu	1,710	1,664	97.31
Urdu	1,07,592	73,051	67.90

Source : Census of India, 1961 *District Census Handbook*, Sehore, p. ixvii.

the major share. Census data for the year 1971 also confirm this trend.[1] We can say that the establishment of the BHEL is largely responsible for changes in the linguistic composition of the population in Bhopal city, as there is only a small possibility for the newly established state capital to attract people speaking different languages from different states.

Changes in workforce structure

Bhopal city not only had a higher percentage of non-agricultural working population but also a higher percentage of the non-household industrial workers compared to the urban areas in the country or the State in 1971. Also it is seen that the city had registered a significant increase in non-household industrial workers compared to the urban areas in the country or the State during sixties. The reason for the lower percentage of non-household industrial workers returned by the city in 1961 is the exclusion of the BHEL township. If we include the BHEL township in Bhopal city, the percentage of non-household to total male workers comes to 25.79 per cent instead of 20.12 per cent in 1961 (Appendix 6.1). Besides, it was noted in from Table 4.1 in the previous chapter that the service sector in Bhopal city was highly developed compared to the urban areas of the country or the State. This may be due to the establishment of the State capital at Bhopal. But undoubtedly the establishment of heavy electrical plant in Bhopal promoted a high rate of industrial growth, as discussed above, which indirectly helped the expansion of the service sector. Again, it can be seen that the city as well as the newly constituted Bhopal district had a higher percentage of male workers compared to the State's urban areas which implies that the workers in Bhopal city are burdened with less number of dependants compared to the workers in the urban areas of the state (Appendix 6.1).

Changes in the educational structure

Over the years, there is a structural change not only in the composition of the work force in Bhopal but also in their educational background. As per the Censuses of 1951, 1961, 1971 and 1981, the literacy rates for Madhya Pradesh are much lower than those of the country. This is true for urban areas of Madhya Pradesh as well (Appendix 6.1). Even a capital city like Bhopal has got lower literacy rate compared to the country's urban areas, although the figure is higher than that of the State. Interestingly, the city as well as the urban areas of Bhopal district had a lower rate of literacy compared to the State in 1961 but over the years, the former had overtaken the latter. This has been possible because of the large number of literate inmigrants during sixties and seventies coupled with the spread of educational facilities in the city and other urban areas of the district. Again, it can be seen from Appendix 5.2 that although the urban area of Sehore district had a lower literacy rate, it had a higher percentage of matriculates, diploma holders, university graduates and technical degree holders like engineers and doctors than the State in 1961 and 1971. Even the educational background of the workers in different occupations is found to be superior in the case of urban areas of Sehore district compared to that of the State (Appendix 5.1). Bhopal city claims more than 85 per cent of the total urban population of Sehore district. As such, Sehore District (urban) having a higher percentage of qualified persons employed in industrial sector as well as in the service sector is not surprising. The employment of more educated and technically qualified workers in the industrial sector as well as in the service sector is primarily due to the establishment of heavy electricals plant and the state capital in Bhopal. Of course, our findings would have been more revealing had we been able to get the data for 1951 also and analysed the change over the subsequent decades.

We know that the urban areas of Sehore district had more than 40 per cent migrants in the years 1961 and 1971 while Bhopal city had more than 50 per cent of its population as migrants, who came from other districts of the State, or from other states of India and foreign countries. It is seen from Appendix 5.2 that the level of literacy among the migrants is comparatively higher than among the total urban population in Sehore district. This process of immigration of literate population (and not of the poor illiterate village folks from the immediate hinterland) helped in increasing the literacy rate in the urban areas of the district. This is also true in the case of the matriculates, degree holders. diploma and technical degree holders who were drawn to the city from far off places. Thus, we can say that with the establishment of the heavy electrical equipment plant in Bhopal, skilled and educated people both from within the State as well as from outside migrated to the city.

Growth of slums in Bhopal city

No doubt the arrival of a large number of migrants from different parts of the country led to significant improvements in the socio-economic characteristics of the population of the Bhopal city, though the influx of the migrants from the impoverished countryside led to the growth of a large number of slums. According to a report of the Bhopal Development Authority, the growth of the slums started on the eve of the establishment of the BHEL unit. Although it was not possible to get information about the emergence of various slum localities at different points of time, we could get some statistics from the Slum Improvement Board, Bhopal. There are presently about 24 slums existing in the city (Fig. 5.1). This is an unintended consequence of urbanisation and industrialisation. This has occurred because the local and the the State Government have failed to provide adequate housing facilities to the poor people coming to the city. Although the Slum Improvement Board does not have any official information regarding the population and households dwelling in slums, according to its officials about 30 per cent of the population in Bhopal city live in slums. In order to find the living conditions of the slum dwellers in Bhopal city, we conducted a field survey of six localities out of the existing 24 slums in Bhopal. As it was not possible to survey each and every household in these six selected localities, we took a sample of 4 per cent of the households. Thus, out of 2,839 households existing in the selected localities we surveyed 115 households by using a questionnaire. Table 5.7 presents the basic information about existing 24 slums in Bhopal whereas the detailed statistics collected through the survey are presented in Appendix 5.3.

In the sample survey, it is found that 44.35 per cent of households belong to scheduled castes and scheduled tribes, of which the scheduled tribes households constitute a very small proportion. In terms of religion, most of the slum dwellers in Bhopal are Hindus (about 74%). The incidence of non-Hindu households varies from locality to locality. Beg Forhat Afja, one of the sample locality has cent per cent non-Hindu households, while the corresponding figures are 46.87 in Sudhama Nagar and 42.86 in Arjun Nagar. The highest percentage of scheduled castes

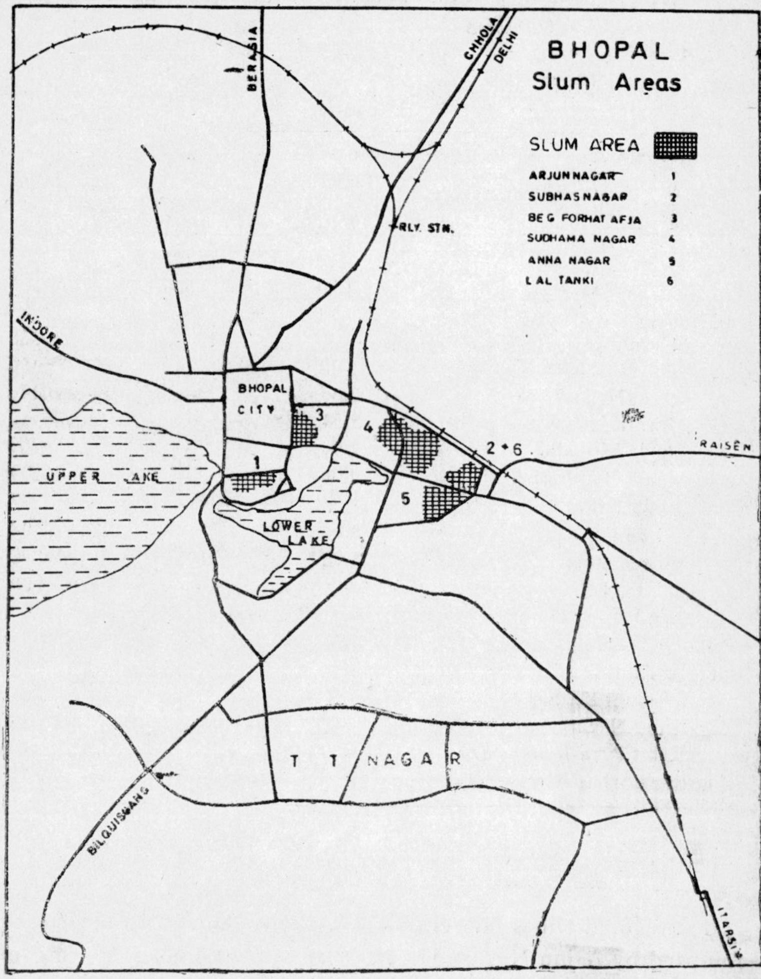
BHOPAL
Slum Areas
SLUM AREA
ARJUN NAGAR 1
SUBHAS NAGAR 2
BEG FORHAT AFJA 3
SUDHAMA NAGAR 4
ANNA NAGAR 5
LAL TANKI 6
BERASIA
CHHOLA
DELHI
RLY. STN.
INDORE
BHOPAL CITY
UPPER LAKE
LOWER LAKE
RAISEN
T T NAGAR
BILQUISGANJ
ITARSI

FIG. 5.1

TABLE 5.7 : **Area, plot and households in the slums of Bhopal city, 1983**

Sl. no.	Name of the locality	Area in acres	No. of plots	No. of households
1.	Pampapur	8.00	264	261
2.	Shiv Nagar	6.00	192	165
3.	Dhobi Ghat	8.00	190	193
4.	Vijay Nagar	11.37	493	410
5.	Shakti Nagar	2.20	123	109
6.	J.P. Nagar	8.80	523	525
7.	Sudhama Nagar*	21.60	1475	788
8.	Narendra Dev Nagar	—	—	688
9.	Subhas Nagar*	5.20	—	186
10.	Arjun Nagar*	3.00	—	176
11.	Morarji Nagar	8.34	—	82
12.	Zhada Mohalla	2.00	—	203
13.	Mandi Berkheri	4.36	—	209
14.	Kushi Pura	11.52	—	7
15.	Lal Ghati	8.00	—	98
16.	Saheed Nagar	8.00	133	270
17.	Lal Tanki*	—	—	600
18.	Bag Umrav Dulha	—	—	—
19.	Khaji Camp	5.57	—	—
20.	Ibrahim Ganj	—	—	—
21.	Khachhi Ka Bag	—	—	—
22.	Anna Nagar	17.00	—	1000
23.	Kabit Pura-Jamal Pura	—	—	—
24.	Beg Forhat Afja*	4.00	—	89

*Slums selected for the primary survey.

Source ; Slum Improvement Board, Bhopal.

and scheduled tribes households is found in Anna Nagar (62.50) followed by Arjun Nagar (57.14). Very few persons from higher castes like Brahmins, Rajputs, Kayasthas or Vaishyas dwell in the slums. Most of the households who live in slums have come to the city from rural areas. About 66.09 per cent of the households have agriculture as their main occupation and most of them are landless agricultural labourers before migrating to the Bhopal city. Among these migrants in our sample, 67.83 per cent are from outside M.P. Among the households coming from other states, it is found that the highest number has come from the backward districts of Maharashtra followed by Uttar Pradesh and Tamil Nadu. It is interesting to note that caste factor has not played a significant role in their settlement pattern in the slums. People of different castes belonging to the same linguistic and regional group are living together in the same locality. For example, in Anna Nagar, people from Maharashtra are living in one *mohalla* and those from Tamil Nadu and Bihar live in some other *mohalla*. Most of the surveyed households (93.91%) are living in the same locality for more than five years. In several cases, we found people living in the same locality for more than 15 years and a number of persons since their birth.

In the sample, more than 50 per cent households have a family size of five and above except in Subhas Nagar where the percentage is 28.57. Thus, the proverbial small family migrant or single person migrant is not very common in the slums of Bhopal city.

It is found that the percentage of population is 42.86 in the age group of 0-14, 53.79 in the age group of 15-59 and 3.35 in the age group of 60 or more. However, these percentages vary from slum to slum. Beg Forhat Afja, for example, has the highest percentage of population in the age group of 0-14 and above 60 years while Arjun Nagar has the highest percentage of adult population in the age group of 15-59 and the lowest percentage in the age-group of 0-14. Compared to the age structure of the population in Bhopal city in 1971 (Appendix 5.4), the slums in 1983 had higher percentage of child population and also of adult population, but a lower percentage of the old. Similarly, compared to the figure of 28.47 per cent workers in the urban areas of Sehore district in 1971, the percentage of workers among slum-dwellers was 34.74 in 1983. The percentage of child workers in the slums was 4.14 in 1983 compared to the percentage of only 1.83 in the city in 1971.[2]

In order to find the proportion of the households in the slums of Bhopal living below the poverty line, an attempt was made to compute the per capita monthly income of the sample households. At the 1977-78 prices, persons with a per capita expenditure of less than Rs. 75 per month are considered to be below the poverty line in the urban areas in India. Allowing for the increase in the cost of living index, persons with an expenditure of less than Rs. 100 per capita per month in 1983 were considered poor in the Bhopal slums. If we follow this criterion, it is seen that 53.91

per cent of the households in our sample slums are living below the poverty line. But the percentage of households living below the poverty line in the localities like Arjun Nagar and Lal Tanki is less compared to other localities in our sample. As a matter of fact, these two localities are adjacent to the BHEL factory. The other three localities that are adjacent to BHEL township have more than 50 per cent of their households below the poverty line. In Subhas Nagar, all the households live below the poverty line and in Beg Forhat Afja, which is in the heart of the old city, about 80 per cent of the persons, who are all Muslims, are poor. It is noted that the localities having a high percentage of the BHEL employees have correspondingly low percentage of households below the poverty line. In Arjun Nagar and Lal Tanki five to six per cent of the total population are BHEL employees compared to 2.82 per cent average figure in our sample slums. Localities like Subhas Nagar and Beg Forhat Afja, where 100 per cent and 80 per cent of the sample households, respectively live below the poverty line, do not have a single BHEL employee in the sample households. These two localities have lower percentage of workers engaged in industries as compared to other localities and have a substantial proportion of the workers engaged as daily labourers in different services such as hotels, restaurants, transport etc.

In our sample slums, about 40.93 per cent workers are engaged in formal industrial units, 24.55 per cent in formal services and 34.71 per cent as daily wage earners. Only 12.17 per cent of the households are self-employed. Households having industrial workers as earners generally have better living conditions than the households with daily wage earners. Although a daily (male) worker in Bhopal city earns about Rs. 10 to 12 per day, this is fairly low in view of the fact that an unskilled worker in informal sector manages to get barely 15 to 20 days of work in a month. As a consequence, their living conditions are much worse than the workers employed in larger industrial units, although their wage rates are the same. It is also observed that 54.78 per cent of the households possess assets worth one thousand rupees or less and only 12.17 per cent households have assets worth more than two thousand rupees. In Arjun Nagar, where the number of households living below the poverty line is quite low, 28.57 per cent of the households possess assets worth more than two thousand rupees. The above findings clearly reveal the extent of poverty among the slum dwellers in Bhopal city.

Persons living in the slums happen to be backward sections of the society both economically as well as educationally. Compared to the city's literacy rate of 56.72 per cent in 1981, only 44.80 per cent of the population in slums are literates in our sample. The slum localities with lower percentage of poor households have higher percentage of literates, as it is normally expected. Also, the slums having a higher percentage of people above the poverty line have a lower literacy rate, except in Beg Forhat Afja. The percentage of graduates and technically qualified population among the literates in the urban areas of Sehore District in 1971 was about five while the corresponding figure for our sample is only 2.19 per cent. With as high as 42.86 per cent child population in the slums, there are only 16.58 per cent school-going children and 1.06 per cent college-going people. As expected, the localities with a higher level of literacy also have a higher percentage of school and college-going population.

On account of the acute poverty and low literacy among the slum-dwellers in Bhopal, the social and physical environment in which they live is not healthy. Although each slum is provided with potable water, there are frequent breakdowns in the supply, due to poor maintenance. There are only a few taps in working condition in each locality. As the supply of water is limited to two to three hours a day, often there are quarrels among housewives and others. Besides water, only four localities have street lighting and of these only Sudhama Nagar has domestic connections and good roads. But in no locality we could find community latrines and bathrooms. In Sudhama Nagar, the municipal authority had provided community latrines long time back but it failed to maintain them. As a result, it has become a source of nuisance for the slum-dwellers. To avail themselves of the medical facilities, people have to walk four to six km. In the case of emergency they fall prey to private doctors as the Government hostpital or dispensary may not admit them. People living in slums adjacent to the BHEL township walk 8 to 10 kms to avail themselves of the medical facilities in the city hospital, as the dispensaries and hospitals located in the BHEL township provide services only to the BHEL employees. Similarly, due to inadequate marketing and other facilities like banks and post offices, they walk half to two km in addition to the distance covered by them every day to go to their place of work. School children also walk a minimum distance of one to two km every day to attend their schools as there is no school in the selected slum localities. At times, the children fail to get admission in Government schools because of their limited strength. As they cannot seek admission in any private school due to high fees etc., a large percentage of these children remain outside the schooling system. The low percentage of the school-going children in the age-group of 0-14 in the selected slums raises serious doubts with regard to Government's performance in achieving the goal of universalisation of elementary education, to be realized by the turn of the century.

The slum dwellers in the Bhopal city presently not only belong to the lowest socio-economic category, they have an extremely pessimistic view regarding their future. The questionnaire sought to find out the willingness of the slum dwellers to raise their own socio-economic status. Only 62 per cent of the sample households feel it necessary to raise their socio-economic conditions. The rest of the population are either satisfied with their present living conditions or chose not to respond to the question. Most of the BHEL employees and Government servants seem to be satisfied with their present jobs as they consider themselves quite well-off compared to the others in their localities. Of the 62 per cent of the households who are willing to improve their socio-economic status, 46.09 per cent desire to open their own workshops or small business, 11.30 per cent prefer occupations like animal husbandry, 0.70 per cent like to get a job in private industries and the remaining 4.35 per cent prefer Government or BHEL jobs. Most of these 62 per cent households desire to have financial support in the form of loan or subsidy from the financial institutions and other Governmental agencies. According to them, banks always ask for security or surety for giving loans. Since they do not possess valuable assets to get the bank loan or circle of friends and relatives to loan the money, it is only Government or voluntary organisations who can help them in cherishing their dreams. These innocent and ignorant people always fall prey to the politicians who promise them regularization of their dwelling units, supply of water and electricity, better educational and medical facilities, interest free loans and financial assistances at the time of election. In Arjun Nagar, it was found that a political party supplied handpumps at the time of election but later removed it by threatening the residents. Also, there are complaints of political leaders taking "donations" from the slum dwellers on the promise of regularising their dwellings and conferring ownership rights which they never do.

From the above discussions, it is clear that there has been structural changes in the socio-economic conditions of Bhopal city since the establishment of the heavy electrical plant. No doubt, the base of industries and service sectors is highly developed in Bhopal and quite a large percentage of the population earn their livelihood from it, but a high rate of migration into the city from impoverished areas of the state and outside has led to the growth of slums as the authorities have failed to provide them with alternate housing facilities. Also, when 30 per cent of the city's population live in slums, there seems to be very limited scope for improving their lot without substantial assistance from the State or Centre. Only recently the Town and Country Planning Organisation and the Bhopal Development Authority including the Slums Improvement Board have taken some steps to rehabilitate a few slum dwellers in a healthy socio-economic environment. However, the high disparity among the population groups within the city has resulted in social tensions and uprisings among the slum dwellers, giving birth to the malignant forces of nativism, regionalism and linguism.

REFERENCES

1. See Census of India, 1971 *Socio-cultural Tables*, Madhya Pradesh.
2. Comparisons have been made between figures at two different points of time as the subsequent census data for the city are not available.

6

BHOPAL AND ITS ENVIRONS—THE SENARIO WITH THE LOCATION OF BHEL UNIT

The concern

One of the important objectives of the Five Year Plans in Ind a has been to remove regional imbalances and achieve sustained and sectorally balanced growth of the economy. As such, the Government of India has kept in view the claims of the relatively backward regions in locating the new public sector enterprises, as far as possible, without disregarding the essential techno-economic feasibility considerations. In the somewhat detailed discussion of the process of the selection of the project site in Chapter 2, it has been brought out that the industry like BHEL, Bhopal with its highly sophisticated technology cannot be located on the ground of backwardness of the region alone, although this was given some weightage in the techno-economic feasibility calculations. No doubt, BHEL, Bhopal has contributed a lot towards the growth and expansion of the power sector in the country. However, it would be interesting to examine whether the industry has got itself integrated with the regional economy and helped in its development. Sometimes, such massive factories create problems of "structural backwardness" in the underdeveloped hinterland through its backwash effects—making the regional imbalances more pronounced over time. In situations like this, the national economy may tend to gain but without the desirable spread effects at the regional level.

Owing to the location of the State Capital and a big public sector project like the BHEL unit, Bhopal is now considered to be an advanced district, as per the classification scheme of the

Madhya Pradesh Government. Bhopal is a new district formed on the 2nd October 1972. It consists of two tahsils, Huzur and Berasia and the district headquarter is located in Bhopal city which comes under Huzur tahsil. Earlier, both the tahsils were parts of Sehore district. Thus, although the present Sehore is a backward district of category 'B', the old district of Sehore which included the present Bhopal district was classified as an advanced district[1] in 1971.

It is seen from the 1981 Census that Bhopal is a highly urbanised district with 76.26 per cent of its population living in urban areas, 75.05 per cent of the population living in Bhopal urban agglomeration alone. It has become one of the advanced districts in the country due to the location of several industries including the BHEL and also the State capital. In fact, the heavy weightage of urban areas has pushed up the level of socio-economic development of the district, notwithstanding the backwardness of the rural areas. It would, therefore, be interesting to study the socio-economic conditions of the rural areas of Bhopal district which has been attempted in the present chapter. An attempt has also been made to assess the impact of BHEL unit on its surrounding rural areas falling within the erstwhile Sehore district during the last three decades.

A comparison of rural and urban areas in Bhopal district

Although Bhopal is a new district constituted after the 1971 Census, it is possible to obtain the figures for different socio-economic indicators for the rural and urban areas of the district by aggregating the values for Huzur and Berasia tahsils from the Census Handbooks of Sehore district of 1961 and 1971 (as Huzur and Berasia tahsils were parts of Sehore district as mentioned above). Since the occupational classification of workers in urban and rural areas throws some light on their levels of socio-economic development, Appendix 6.1 has been prepared using 1961, 1971 and 1981 Census data articulating the occupational structure of the workforce. In order to draw inferences regarding the relative levels, the data for Madhya Pradesh and India have been taken alongwith the data for Bhopal district and its two tahsils.

The present Bhopal district happens to be the most urbanised district of the State with 61.66, 68.72 and 76.26 per cent of its total population living in urban areas in the Census years of 1961, 1971 and 1981 respectively. This compares very favourably with Madhya Pradesh's urban population of 14.29 per cent in 1961, 16.29 per cent in 1971 and 20.31 per cent in 1981. The comparative figures for the country are 17.97 per cent in 1961, 19.91 per cent in 1971 and 23.71 per cent in 1981. The rates of population growth in urban areas was quite high *viz.*, 71·32 per cent during 1961-71 and 73.99 per cent during 1971-81 in the case of Bhopal district whereas the corresponding growth in the case of Madhya Pradesh was 46.63 per cent during 1961-71 and 56.07 per cent during 1971-81 only. Contrary to this, the growth rates of population in rural areas was 25.96 per cent during 1961-71 and 18.44 per cent during 1971-81 in Bhopal district. These are almost equal to the corresponding figures for the State. Besides, it is to be noted that the rural areas of the Huzur tahsil registered a very low rate of population growth (7.01%) during 1971-81. This is due to the expansion of the urban limits of Bhopal city and not due to the large scale migration of population from rural to the urban areas. But in the other tahsil of the district the picture is quite different. The rural areas of Berasia tahsil registered an impressive population growth rate of 28.92 per cent. The rural (and also urban) sex ratio (the number of females per thousand males) is quite low in Bhopal district compared to the State and the country. This clearly indicates that the rate of out-migration of males from rural areas (which pushes up the sex ratio) to urban areas in Bhopal district is quite low. However, the sex ratio in the urban areas of Bhopal district is still lower, because of the large number of male in-migrants into the urban centres—largely into Bhopal city from outside the district and the State.

It is observed in Appendix 6.1 that the percentages of male workers in the primary sector in rural India were 80.09 and 84.15 in 1961 and 1971, respectively. In Madhya Pradesh, the figures were 86.98 and 87.63 ; in Bhopal district—83.09 and 91.88 ; in Berasia tahsil—87.36 and 94.23 and in Huzur tehsil—78.36 and 86.47. From the above statistics it can be said that the rural areas of the Bhopal district have come to depend more on agriculture. Although the share of agricultural workers has increased in the rural areas of Madhya Pradesh (as well as in India), the rise here is relatively less steep. The corresponding increases for Berasia and Huzur tahsils are very high. This clearly indicates that during the decade 1961-71 the rural areas of Bhopal district did not experience sectoral diversification in response to the growth of industrial activities in the urban areas. Moreover, while the percentage of male workers in the non-household industries registered an increase over the years 1961 and 1971 in the rural areas of Madhya Pradesh and India as a whole, the rural areas of Bhopal district as well as Huzur tahsil, showed a significant fall in this percentage, notwithstanding the presence of the big public sector unit like BHEL and several other industrial units in their close proximity. There was a substantial fall in the percentage of male workers in the tertiary sector also during the sixties along with a high rate of growth of male workers in the primary sector. These cannot be explained in terms of the migration of male non-household and tertiary sector workers in large numbers to the industrial areas of Bhopal. This is because the rural population in Bhopal district as well as in Huzur tahsil have experienced a very fast growth rate compared to Madhya Pradesh and the country as a whole. This establishes that net out-migration of population from rural areas to urban areas in the district was marginal.

It is generally expected that with industrialisation and urbanisation in a backward region, the lower sections of the society i.e. scheduled caste and scheduled tribe population would migrate to the urban industrial centres—to settle down in the less repressive social milieu. But in the case of rural areas of Bhopal district or Huzur tahsil, this has not happened. Similarly, the literacy level in the rural areas of Bhopal district had not shown any significant increase during the decade 1961-71 compared to the country or the state. Also, the rural and urban areas of the district showed very little increase in the literacy rate during the decade 1971-81 compared to the increase in Madhya Pradesh and the country as a whole.

It may be inferred from Appendix 6.1 that during 1971-81 the rural areas of Bhopal district showed a distinct increase in the percentage of male cultivators when the rural areas of Madhya Pradesh and India as a whole registered a marginal fall. Also, in the case of male agricultural labourers in rural areas there was a significant fall in the percentage figure for the district during the above period, while the fall in this figure for Madhya Pradesh and India was only marginal. But on the whole, the percentage of workers deriving their livelihood from agriculture in rural areas of Bhopal district was quite high (87.03%) in 1981 in comparison to the rural areas of Madhya Pradesh (85.17%) and India (79.52%). Similarly, in the case of male household industrial workers in the rural areas for the year 1981, for which data are available it is noted that contrary to the marginal changes in the figures for Madhya Pradesh and India during 1971-81, the rate of decline for Bhopal district was quite significant. It can, therefore, be stated that although the urban areas of Bhopal district had shown relative socio-economic prosperity over the years from 1961 to 1981, the rural areas of the district had not benefited much and in some cases these had become worse off during this period.

It is not only the rural areas of the Bhopal district that have shown deterioration in their socio-economic conditions, the rural economy of the Sehore district also showed negative features of development during 1961-71, unlike the urban areas of the district. It has been said earlier that the undivided district of Sehore which included the newly constituted Bhopal district was considered a relatively developed district in 1971. But the percentage of male workers deriving their livelihood from the primary sector were 85.15 per cent and 89.55 per cent in the rural areas of Sehore district in 1961 and 1971, respectively. It may be noted that the proportion of workers in the primary sector increased at a much faster rate in Sehore than in the country or the State. It is, thus clear that Sehore was categorised as an advanced district not because of an integrated growth of rural and urban areas of the district but mainly due to the growth of Bhopal City, partially at the cost of its hinterland.

BHEL, Bhopal and its impact on the periphery—the village survey

A survey of 24 villages located (Fig. 6.1) around the BHEL factory and the Bhopal city was conducted in February-March, 1983 through a village level questionnaire with the objective of assessing the impact of the BHEL unit on its surrounding region. The time frame of the study did not permit a household level survey in these villages.

It has been discussed earlier that in the Huzur tahsil, where the city of Bhopal as well as the BHEL factory is located, the percentage of male workers in the rural areas engaged in the

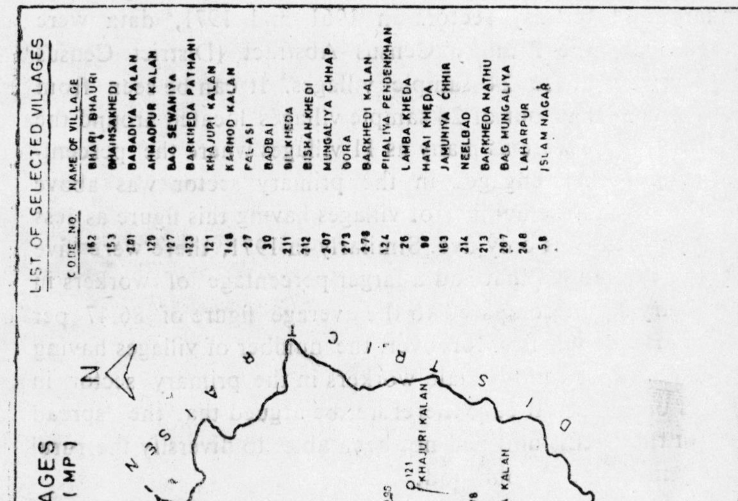
LOCATION OF SELECTED VILLAGES
HUZUR TAHSIL DISTRICT SEHORE (MP)
TAHSIL BERASIA
BHOPAL
ISLAM NAGAR
KHAJURI KALAN
BABADIYA KALAN
MUNGALIYA CHHAP
BHAUNRI
SEHORE
LEGEND
URBAN AREA
SMALL VILLAGE
BIG VILLAGE
LIST OF SELECTED VILLAGES
CODE NO. NAME OF VILLAGE
182 BHARI BHAURI
153 BHAINSAKHEDI
281 BABADIYA KALAN
129 AHMADPUR KALAN
127 BAO SEWANIYA
123 BARKHEDA PATHANI
121 KHAJURI KALAN
148 KARHOD KALAN
27 PALASI
30 BADBAI
211 BILKHEDA
212 BISHANKHEDI
207 MUNGALIYA CHHAP
273 DORA
278 BARKHEDI KALAN
124 PIPALIYA PENDENKHAN
26 LAMBA KHEDA
98 HATAI KHEDA
163 JAMUNIYA CHHIR
214 NEELBAD
213 BARKHEDA NATHU
287 BAG MUNGALIYA
288 LAHARPUR
58 ISLAM NAGAR

FIG. 6.1

primary sector was 78.36 in 1961 and 86.47 in 1971. In order to find out whether the sampled villages located around the BHEL unit and Bhopal city within a radius of 15 to 20 km were different from the rural areas of Huzur tahsil in terms of the number of people deriving their livelihood from the primary, secondary and tertiary sectors in 1961 and 1971, data were collected from the Primary Census Abstract (District Census Handbook) for these 24 sample villages. It can be seen from Appendix 6.2 that out of 24 sample villages located around the BHEL unit, there were as many as 11 villages where the percentage of male workers engaged in the primary sector was above 78.36 in 1961 and the number of villages having this figure as less than 70 per cent was only five. Similarly in 1971, there were five villages in the sample that had a larger percentage of workers in the primary sector compared to the average figure of 86.47 per cent for Huzur tahsil. Moreover. the number of villages having less than 70 per cent of male workers in the primary sector in 1971 was only four. It can, therefore, be argued that the 'spread effect' of the BHEL unit had not been able to diversify the rural economy in the neighbourhood.

In sixteen villages of the sample, the percentage of male workers engaged in the household industry showed a slower decline than the rural areas of Huzur tahsil during 1961-71. There was also a general decline in the percentage of male non-household workers in the rural areas of Huzur tahsil. However, in the case of the sample villages, the picture is not very clear. Whereas in half of the villages the percentage of workers in the corresponding category has risen, in the remaining it has gone down. In the construction sector also, as many as nine sample villages showed a relatively faster decline of male workers compared to the rural areas of Huzur tahsil. So, one cannot say definitely that there is a spread effect within the region and a number of industries are coming up through 'multiplier impact' around the BHEL unit in the rural areas.

Apart from that, seventeen of the sample villages showed a higher percentage of literacy than that of the rural areas of Huzur tahsil in 1971. However, the average literacy rate in the case of rural areas of Huzur tahsil was relatively lower than the average literacy rate of the rural areas of the district, the state of Madhya Pradesh and the country, in the Census years of 1971 and

1981. Moreover, the remaining seven villages of the sample had a very low literacy rate compared to the average literacy rate of the rural areas in Huzur tahsil. One can, therefore, argue that despite their proximity to the capital city with a cosmopolitan character, these sample villages in the periphery failed to register a high literacy rate over the years. Similarly, there has been an increase in the percentage of SC and ST population on most of the sampled villages. This does not confirm the thesis of out migration of males and SC/ST population from the periphery to the centre nor that of declining population in the rural areas due to the operation of strong pull factors. Conspicuously, lower number of females per thousand males in the sample villages as well as in the rural areas of Huzur tahsil and Bhopal district compared to the rural areas of the State proves that the urban centres have failed to attract large number of male migrants from their periphery. The over-all rate of increase in population in these villages indicates that depopulation of the periphery due to urban pull has not occurred. It is true that a few villages in the sample registered negative growth rate during the decade 1961-1971, but this was due to the inclusion of their areas in the municipal boundaries of Bhopal city. On the other hand, the trend of population growth in the peripheral rural areas confirms that periphery is becoming overpopulated as the city is unable to absorb the large scale influx of migrants.

Despite the location of state capital and a huge public sector unit like the BHEL in Bhopal, the periphery had a very low level of infrastructural facilities as indicated by the Census data of 1971 (Appendix 6.3). The rural areas of Huzur tehsil had a very low proportion of irrigated land in 1971-72 *viz*, 1.81 per cent of total area and 3.68 per cent of the net area sown, whereas the state and the country had 8.90 per cent and 22.80 per cent of irrigated land to net area sown in 1973-74. In our sample, fifteen out of 24 villages had less than 1.82 per cent of irrigated land to total land area. Despite their proximity to the city of Bhopal and the BHEL unit, only six villages in the sample had middle school facilities and thirteen villages had primary school facilities in 1971. None of the villages in the sample had a high school and four villages did not have any educational facility. With regard to medical facilities also, the sample villages seemed to be at a disadvantage compared to the average rural settlement in the

State. In 1971, there was only one family planning centre functioning at one of the sample villages i.e. Hataikheda. Similarly, only ten villages in the sample had electricity in 1971 and only six had electricity connection for industry and irrigation. However, the sample villages had a distinct advantage over the others in Huzur tahsil in regard to facilities *like pucca* road and electricity. Although only 28.77 per cent villages had *pucca* road and 11.88 per cent villages had electricity in Huzur tahsil in 1971, the comparative figures for the sample villages were, 58.33 per cent and 37.50 per cent, respectively.

The above analysis of 24 sample villages using data from the Censuses of 1961 and 1971 indicates that the villages around the BHEL unit and Bhopal city experienced both 'backwash and spread effects', the former outweighing the latter in most cases. However, it is not possible to say from the above analysis of the census data whether the deterioration in the peripheral areas was mainly due to the location of the BHEL unit. In assessing the impact of the BHEL, results of the primary survey of these 24 villages, as discussed above, would be extremely useful. The statistical data compiled through the survey are presented in Appendices 6.4 and 6.5.

It is seen from Appendix 6.4 that out of 24 villages, 12 villages have a sizeable percentage of scheduled caste and scheduled tribe population which is more than the national average of 22 per cent in 1971. However, these villages are predominated by the scheduled caste population and the number of scheduled tribe households in the sample villages is very low. At the time of the village survey, it was noted that there were 9 villages in the sample which had a population of more than one thousand. However, the 1971 Census reports only 4 villages in the sample as having a population above one thousand. Further, it was found that almost all villages in the sample registered a higher increase in population during the period 1971-81 compared to that of the (rural) country, State, district or tahsil whose growth figures were 18.96 per cent, 19.16 per cent, 18.44 per cent and 7.01 per cent, respectively. In our sample, there was not a single village which did not register a growth rate of more than 30 per cent in its population during the decade 1971-81. The higher growth of population coupled with adverse sex ratio in these peripheral villages is mainly due to the influx of immigrant population, usually consisting of male migrants. Possibly, the large number of immigrants to Bhopal city find it difficult to get suitable accommodation inside the city and these people have started spreading out into the peripheral villages.

The composition of the labour force presented in Appendix 6.4 shows that most of the households in our sample villages derive their livelihood from agriculture. In as many as 14 villages, it has been found that the agricultural labour and daily wage earning households outweigh the peasant cultivator households. From the findings of the village survey, it can be inferred that most of the households in these villages are still attached to agriculture and allied activities. The households dependent on the primary sector are more than 85 per cent. However, the existing infrastructural facilities for the development of agriculture and allied activities are so low that there is hardly any scope for the improvement of productivity that could raise the standard of living. The pressure of population on land is very high and the landholding structure is highly unequal. It is skewed in favour of the rich and higher castes. Besides, due to the acquisition of cultivable land from the peripheral villages at the time of the construction of the BHEL factory and its township, the per capita availability of land in many of these villages is lower than the average per capita availability of 0.24 hectare of land in India.

As per the 1971 Census, the villages in the sample had less than 50 per cent of their total land under cultivation. The information given by the people in the nearby villages of the BHEL factory, such as Pipaliya Pendenkhan, Bag-Mungaliya, Bag-Sewaniya, Laharpur, Barkheda Pathani, Khajuri Kalan and Hataikheda etc., indicate that these villages lost considerable portion of their cultivable land due to the construction of BHEL factory and township. At the time of acquisition of land, the amount of compensation paid to the villages was lower than the existing market value and nobody could purchase land in some other places using the compensation money, or switch over to any other occupation. Most of the villagers relied on the promises made by the project authority that at least one member of each household that had lost cultivable land would be provided with a job in the factory in due course. Unfortunately, only a few of them could get jobs in the BHEL factory. Consequently, being illiterates, most of these small and marginal farmers were reduced to the status of landless agricultural labourers and daily-wage earners, as they failed to get absorbed in the emerging urban industrial sector of Bhopal.

It is not only that a few of the villages located around the Factory lost their cultivable land but, in fact, many more lost their land with the expansion of Bhopal lake undertaken to supply water to the BHEL township and also to the increasing population of Bhopal city. In total, as many as fifteen villages in the sample are found to have lost their cultivable land ranging from hundred to thousand acres. The amount of compensation paid to the people was very low as mentioned above. Moreover, the people who lost their land due to the expansion of the lake were not provided any job, as was attempted in the case of those losing land to the BHEL.

Agriculture, which is the mainstay of the people in these villages, is found to be in a precarious state. Owing to the higher pressure of population on land alongwith the traditional methods of cultivation, the productivity of land happens to be very low. People in these villages grow traditional crops like rice, wheat, jowar, bajra, chana, masoor etc. Only a small fraction of the peasantry has switched over, that too recently, to cash crops like soyabean, sunflower seed etc. The agrarian economy at these villages has, thus, remained subsistence oriented, i e. whatever is produced in the villages is largely consumed by them. Traditional pattern of cultivation and unequal land distribution coupled with the loss of agricultural land left majority of the households with uneconomic landholdings. As a consequence, despite expanded irrigation facilities provided through electrification of villages, people in general have not been able to benefit from them. Most of these villages in the sample are electrified primarily for irrigation purpose.

However, the small and marginal farmers have failed to benefit from these irrigational facilities due to the lack of easy accessibility to capital. There is hardly any impact of the Integrated Rural Development Programme (IRDP) or the National Rural Employment Programme (NREP) on these villages. The prevalence of widespread illiteracy among the villagers coupled with an indifferent attitude of the bureaucrats towards rural development has kept the agrarian economy at a very low level of development. The facilities of institutional finance provided to small and marginal farmers through IRDP, MFAL programme etc., for the adoption of modern technology and inputs hardly reached the real target groups. The poor people in the villages do not have easy access to credit institutions like cooperative credit societies, regional rural banks etc. Moreover, most of these surveyed villages have land brought under the municipal boundary of Bhopal in recent years. Consequently, the condition of the rural economy in these villages have become worse as these are neither counted as a part of the city of Bhopal nor as villages.

The impact of the modern scientific farming and the gains accruing from it, although very limited, have been monopolized by only a small section of the cultivators. In most of the villages surveyed, it was found that only two or three households belonging to the higher castes and often from the same family were controlling more than seventy per cent of the cultivable land and the rest of the households in the village were subservient to them in some way or the other. The landowners belonging to the higher income groups use high yielding varieties of seeds and chemical fertilizers and have adopted capitalist farming by using tractors and other modern agricultural implements like threshers, harvesters and winnowers. Besides the concentration of agricultural lands in the hands of the traditional higher caste families, it was found that the marginal and small farmers in these villages had been alienated forcibly from their land over the past few years due to large scale indebtedness caused by the unforeseen eventualities like droughts, famines and other familial crises. In some cases, it was found that the prosperous outsiders living in Bhopal city or the traditional village landlord-cum-money lenders have grabbed the land of small and marginal farmers when the latter have sunk into indebtedness. Consequently, most of the small and marginal farmers in these villages have been pauperised in this process of lopsided development and the mechanization of agriculture resulting in the displacement of agricultural labourers.

Besides agriculture, a few households in these villages have adopted dairy farming as their main subsidiary occupation whereas a few others grow vegetables. The BHEL township and Bhopal city provide them with a good market. However, despite the high demand for vegetables, milk and milk products in the BHEL locality and also in Bhopal city, these activities have not developed satisfactorily due to the lack of pasture and cultivable land. For most of the households these activities have remained a subsidiary occupation in addition to agriculture. The activities like dairy farming, poultry, animal husbandry, growing of vegetables, pisciculture, horticulture etc., are not picking up in these villages due to the scarcity of land and the capital, although labour is abundant in these villages. Not a single household in the sample villages has adopted poultry farming as its occupation and very few have gone in for animal husbandry, despite the high demand for eggs, fish, and meat in Bhopal city.

Similarly, the non-agricultural activities in these villages are in a very sad state. There is hardly any development of the cottage industry even in the big villages having a population of more than one thousand. On the other hand, the number of persons deriving their livelihood from the household industry has gone down significantly over the years, as indicated by the census data of these villages. Persons dependent on the tertiary sectors like trade and commerce, transport, communication etc., are also much less now than before ten to fifteen years. Of course, one may attempt to explain this in terms of migration of able bodied villagers to Bhopal city. However, the high growth of population in these villages coupled with the adverse sex ratio discounts the contention (out-migrating villages tend to have a high sex ratio). One can argue that the fall in non-agricultural activities in these villages is not primarily due to the male selective outmigration from the periphery to the centre. Despite rapid industrialisation in Bhopal city, very few people from the peripheral villages are found having formal employment in its expanding tertiary and secondary sectors. The only gain which the peripheral villages seem to have got due to the location of BHEL unit is in terms of a few lower category jobs. The field data revealed that only about 415 people from these villages have found employment in the BHEL factory and that too in the category of semi-skilled and unskilled workers. Among these, only three were artisans, one was a foreman and none held an executive post. As discussed in Chapter 4, the BHEL unit is directly responsible for the growth of about 50 per cent of the engineering and electrical goods industries and at least 30 per cent of the total employment in the secondary sector in Bhopal city. However, besides these 415 people, there are not more than fifty persons who have found employment in the other industrial units in Bhopal. The total population of our sample villages will not be less than 18 thousand and the number of working population will be above eight thousand in 1983. Compared to this workforce, the number of persons employed in the industrial sector is very low. It is noted that in seven sample villages *viz.*, Bhaunri, Gora, Bishan Khedi, Barkhedi Kalan, Neelbad, Barkheda Nathu and Karhod Kalan, there is not even a single worker employed in the BHEL factory. In other cases, a few persons have found employment in the BHEL factory although most of them are employed as semi-skilled or unskilled workers. An unskilled or a semi-skilled worker in BHEL earns a monthly salary between Rs. 600 and Rs. 1,000 with a regular flow of income. As most of the persons working in this category belong to the weaker sections of the society, it may be said that the location of the BHEL unit in Bhopal has helped a few poor people in the neighbouring villages. However, it is seen from Appendices 6.4 and 6.5 that the number of persons employed in BHEL is relatively high in the case of the adjacent villages within a distance of 10 km of the city. The villages located beyond a distance of 15 km, however, felt little impact of the factory, as is the case of the seven villages in the sample mentioned above.

The existing infrastructural facilities in the sample villages are found to be relatively more developed than the normal villages in Huzur tahsil. While only 28.77 per cent villages were connected by the *pucca* road in Huzur tahsil in 1971, 58.33 per cent of sample villages had *pucca* roads. Similarly, compared to the electrification of only 11.88 per cent villages in the tahsil in 1971, 37.50 per cent of sample villages were electrified. At the time of the survey, it was found that 21 of the 24 villages were provided with electricity (i.e. 87.50%). The educational facilities available in the rural areas of Huzur tahsil, Bhopal district and Sehore district, appear to be much less than in the sample villages, as may be inferred from the literacy rates and number of schools in these villages in 1971. At the time of the village survey in 1983, there was only one village in the sample which did not have even a primary school. Seven villages had middle schools and two villages namely, Mungaliya Chhap and Barkheda Nathu had a high school each. However, as discussed earlier, the literacy rates, the number of graduates and technically qualified persons were not very high in these villages as one would expect because of their nearness to the capital city and the industrial township. Similarly, compared to other villages in the State, district or tahsil, the sample villages had better access to medical facilities. It was noted during the survey that two government managed dispensaries were functioning in the villages of Hataikheda and Mungaliya Chhap. There were also two private clinics at Karhod Kalan and Islam Nagar. Besides these, majority of the villages had an easy access to the hospitals in Bhopal city.

Despite this relatively higher level of certain infrastructural facilities, the economic conditions of the villagers seem to have deteriorated over the years. Although 60 per cent of the sample villages are connected by *pucca* roads, adequate transport facility is not available to the rural population to commute to Bhopal city to earn thier livelihood. The villages connected to the city by *kutcha* roads become almost inaccessible during the rainy season. The electrification of the villages in the periphery has neither helped in increasing the agricultural productivity by increasing the intensity of cropping, irrigation etc., nor has it helped the development of agro-based industries. Given the limited cultivable land with highly unequal agrarian structure, the large scale dependence on the primary sector has been responsible for the deteriorating living conditions of the villagers. Most of the households are poverty-ridden, surrounding a few affluent households. Besides the few rich land owning persons, only a few BHEL and other state government employees have a permanent source of income. Not many people at the lower socio-economic strata are found to have improved their living conditions with the establishment of a big public sector unit like BHEL. Most of the villagers feel that their living conditions were far better before the establishment of BHEL factory. They argue that before the establishment of the factory, almost everybody in the village had a few acres of cultivable land to earn their livelihood. But the establishment of massive public sector project resulted in the loss of their cultivable as well as pasture land. As most of the displaced people in these villages failed to get an alternate employment, the pressure of population on the land increased tremendously. Furthermore, due to the loss of pasture land, very few households in these villages could switch over to allied occupations like dairy farming, pisciculture, poultry farming, animal husbandry etc.. Apart from that, the State government or the project authority (i.e. BHEL) have not undertaken the responsibility of imparting technical training to the rural folk—especially those displaced from their land. The people in these villages have a feeling that they have been discriminated against by the management of BHEL as the most of the middle and higher level positions went to the outsiders. They feel that most of the other benefits of the BHEL factory are also cornered by the outsiders due to lack of awareness among the local people. Due to the slow progress in agriculture, the working class in these villages hardly get 150 days of employment in a year and the existing wage rate fixed up by the State government is scarcely accepted by the employers.

Many people interviewed during the survey complained that they had been pauperised due to the increasing industrialisation and urbanisation in the Bhopal region. Most of these people thought that recently they had come to face scarcity of the basic necessities of life, like drinking water, fuel etc. This is often attributed to the industrialisation and urbanisation in the region resulting in the denudation of forest land, large scale erosion of the soil and cumulative environmental pollution.

Based on the above analysis, it may be concluded that the BHEL factory and the emerging industrial sector in Bhopal have both positive and negative impact on the region, the latter outweighing the former. It seems that the spread effect of the BHEL factory is limited to the immediate hinterland. The influence of the factory seems to taper off with distance and beyond 15 km from the project site the negative impact is noted to be far more serious. In terms of BHEL jobs, the sample villages have got a weak support from the factory and the villagers who have succeeded in finding employment in the factory are either semi-skilled or un-skilled labourers. The selling of milk and milk products, vegetables and food grains etc., in the BHEL locality by the people from the nearby villages is present but only at a very low level and its growth is hampered by the high cost of transport and the irregular transport service. This is responsible for the emergence of the merchant class or the middlemen who make very high profits and exploit the poor peasants. However, observations at the time of survey and informal interviews with the villagers revealed that a large number of villagers had adopted urban modes of living. There is significant demonstration effect on the rural folks in the periphery and their consumption pattern is changing very fast, although the income opportunities are not growing perceptively over time.

Relatively higher growth rate of population during the last couple of decades in the sample villages and also in the rural areas of Huzur and Berasia tahsils indicates large scale in-migration. This may seem curious as there are not much employment opportunities within the village. It is obvious that a large number of people seeking employment in Bhopal city are working in various informal sectors. They cannot afford a residential accommodation within the city and consequently live in hutments and shanties in the villages. This has initiated a process of *degenerated peripheralisation*[2], which is characteristic of most of the metropolitan cities in India. It was observed at the time of the survey that there was a high rate of unemployment including educated unemployment in these villages.

Despite the development of a number of capital intensive industries in Bhopal region, it seems that the human capital in the periphery is very backward. The closeness of the villages to the state capital and its emergence as a major industrial township encouraged very few young people to go in for college or university education, not to speak of the technical education in engineering, medical colleges, polytechnics and ITI. The high rate of unemployment among the educated persons including the vocationally trained persons perhaps discouraged people in these villages to acquire higher education. Although the social disease like untouchability in these villages seems to have gone down considerably, the other evils like repression of women folk, child marriages etc., are rampant. The spread of women education is also quite low in these villages.

It seems from the above analysis that BHEL in Bhopal with its ancillaries and other interlinked small scale units has not been able to transmit growth impulses to the surrounding region. No doubt a few industrial units in the Bhopal region have come up due to the backward linkages of BHEL unit but the factory and its ancillary units do not utilise much of the resources of the region including the labour force and the entrepreneurship. The raw-materials which they require come from different parts of India and the products they produce are sold and utilised throughout the country and in a few cases they are even exported to foreign countries. The real development of the periphery would have taken place if the BHEL unit had helped the development of infrastructural facilities and the formation of human capital in the region. But the apathy of the state apparatus and the indifference of the bureaucrats came in the way as a major obstacle. Consequently, the periphery has shown distinct signs of backwash effects exerted by the big public sector unit with marginal spread effects. Thus, while from the national perspective, BHEL, Bhopal can be said to have contributed a lot, for the Bhopal region it has remained more or less a liability, creating an enclave of dysfunctional development surrounded by the ocean of structural backwardness. Due to the high fares and lack of regular bus services, it is very difficult for the villagers to commute to the city or nearby villages every day to earn bread and during the rainy season this becomes impossible. The BHEL factory hardly utilises any resource of the region except the land where it is located. The raw materials which it requires come from different parts of India and its products are sold throughout the country, as mentioned above. A few industrial units have come up in the city and its periphery, thanks to the backward linkages of the BHEL unit, supplying inputs to the latter. However, no unit worth the name has come up having forward linkages with the BHEL factory, units that use the output of the BHEL as inputs in their production process. One would, therefore, not be wrong in holding that though BHEL, Bhopal has contributed a lot towards the national economic development, for the immediate region it has remained a sort of liability.

REFERENCES

1. The forty-five districts of Madhya Pradesh have been divided into two categories—advanced and backward. The backward districts have been further divided into three categories—A, B and C as per the degree of backwardness, in the descending order.
2. See Kundu, A. "City for the Elite", *The Statesman*, 13 Dec., 1985.

7

BHEL AND THE DEVELOPMENT OF BHOPAL REGION—AN ASSESSMENT

THE BHEL unit of Bhopal is the first and the largest heavy electrical equipment plant in India. It is one of the eight factories in the world that manufacture at one place, the whole range of large equipments for generation, transmission and utilization of electric power. BHEL, Bhopal started production in 1960-61 with a meagre output of Rs. 0.21 crore and in the year 1981-82 it recorded an out-turn of Rs. 198 crore. Since its inception in 1960-61 to the end of year 1981-82, its cumulative production (finished) has been Rs. 1,374 crore at current prices. Again, within a period of eight years of its existence, it penetrated into export market in 1968-69 with an order from UAR worth Rs. 1.73 lakh and till the year 1981-82, it executed cumulative order of Rs. 59.39 crore. This is not a small achievement in view of the competition faced by a heavy electrical plant in a developing country against the big multinationals, with their high technology products. As we discussed in Chapter 3, the financial performance of the BHEL Corporate Sector was far better than that of the public sector enterprises as a whole and the former had generated considerable investible resources since the year 1971-72. Similarly, BHEL had taken two sick units which were its subsidiaries, namely, Radio and Electrical Manufacturing Company (REMCO) and Mysore Porcelain Limited (MPL) under its control in May 1980 in order to retain the employees. In promoting and establishing ancillary units, the BHEL Corporate Sector as a whole has played a very important role. In the year 1980-81, BHEL had 137 ancillary units located in Bhopal, Jhansi, Hardwar, Hyderabad and Tiruchi. Of these, BHEL, Bhopal had as many as fifty-two.[1] Besides, it has become a pioneer in the industrial development of the country by contributing more than 80 per cent of the power producing equipments like thermal power sets, hydro sets etc., for the generation of additional power in recent years. In the year 1980-81, the share of BHEL equipment was 42.4 per cent of the total installed capacity, i.e. 12,728 MW out of 30,000 MW, in the country. Thus, BHEL as a whole and the BHEL unit of Bhopal in particular have fulfilled one of the major objectives of the Public Sector in India, i.e. the promotion of overall economic development in the country.

It has been mentioned above that the oldest and the biggest heavy electrical equipment plant in the country was finally chosen to be located in Bhopal not only on the ground of backwardness of the region but because it satisfied the major technical requirements of the site, as recommended by the Consultants, AEI of U.K., out of 14 selected sites in different states of the country. Also BHEL, Bhopal serves the development needs of the entire industrial sector, agricultural sector and the service sector by expanding the power base of the country. The efficiency of the BHEL, Bhopal is, therefore, not to be judged in terms of the development of the regional economy alone but also in terms of the development of the national economy. Nevertheless, when a big industry in the public sector is established in a region, it is likely to have both positive as well as negative impact on its economy. We know that one of the objectives of the BHEL is to make it act as an instrument of social change through its policies, products, service facilities, plans and schedules, and through the various social, civic and economic responsibilities it has taken upon itself.

The pattern of industrial growth in Bhopal shows that about 50 per cent of the units belonging to the engineering, electrical and electronic industries have come up due to the existence of the BHEL unit. When a big industrial unit is established in a region, it develops the basic infrastructure like transport, communication, power and marketing facilities. Subsequently, many small scale units grow due to the patronisation by the big units through its forward and backward linkages. Similarly, because of the relatively higher wages earned by the workers in the public enterprises, the living standard of workers tends to go up. Indirectly, it helps the agricultural sector in the region by absorbing a part of its disguisedly unemployed labour force. The increase in income of the workers creates more demand for consumer goods. This, subsequently, results in the growth of consumer goods industries in the region. We saw in Chapter 4 that there was not only the growth of capital goods industries in the Bhopal region but also a high growth of consumer goods industries and this was higher than the corresponding growth rate for the State during the decade 1961-1971. Similarly, compared to the statutory minimum wage rate of Rs. 7.10 per day for unskilled workers, the minimum wages in Bhopal city ranges between Rs. 10 and Rs. 12 per day. Again we could see that Bhopal city as well as the urban areas in Sehore district had more than 25 per cent non-household male industrial workers (to the total workers) in 1971 compared to the State and country's figure of only 20 per cent and 24 per cent, respectively. This clearly suggests a steady process of industrial growth in Bhopal. Besides, the BHEL unit makes purchases worth more than Rs. 6 crore in a year from small scale units located in Indore, Jabalpur, Dewas, Gwalior etc., within the State and from places like Delhi, Bombay, Calcutta, Madras, Ghaziabad, Jhansi, Ludhiana, Hyderabad, Vijayawada, Faridabad, Bangalore etc., outside the State, as shown by the purchase record of the subcontracting divisions of BHEL, Bhopal. We can, therefore, say that the BHEL unit of Bhopal has encouraged the growth of small scale units in different parts of the State and the country.

In Chapter 5, it was observed that there had been significant changes in the socio-economic conditions of the city because of the location of the BHEL unit. There was large scale migration from different parts of M.P. and other states to Bhopal city during 1961-71, a portion of them came from different parts of Sehore district. This massive influx of migrants has given the city and its region a different colour. Not only the BHEL township, the city of Bhopal itself looks like a mini-India with people belonging to different cultures, religions and linguistic regions, living together simultaneously in a cosmopolitan environment.

Despite these developments, our survey of the 24 villages around Bhopal city brings out some of the negative features of the development. The villages around Bhopal city continue to be as backward as these were before 1961. There is hardly any spread of development in the neighbouring rural areas. Till now, the villages around Bhopal are inaccessible due to the lack of proper communication facilities. Most of the villages do not have drinking water facilities. A large number of them remain unelectrified, although they lie within a distance of 10 km from the factory, producing heavy electrical equipments. The villages having schools do not have school buildings to create a proper learning environment. Although all these villages fall within the capital region, only a few like Karhod Kalan, Lambakheda etc., are connected with Bhopal by good roads. Many of the villages do not have a significant number of high school going children, not to speak of college going students. The weaker sections of the society *viz.*, scheduled castes, scheduled tribes and female population seem to be totally neglected in the spheres of education. In the 24 surveyed villages, there are very few girl students attending middle school. The general level of literacy in these villages is also quite low compared to the city. On the other hand, there is an increasing feeling among the people in these villages that they are being neglected because of the importance given to Bhopal city. They feel that the loss of their cultivable land due to the location of BHEL factory and the township, the expansion of the city boundary and the Bhopal lake has not been adequately compensated. The amount of money paid to these villagers was so low that they could hardly afford to develop culturable wasteland or purchase land in nearby areas. In these villages, more than 90 per cent of the population derive their livelihood from agriculture. Due to the loss of their cultivable land, the villagers feel that they were robbed off their livelihood by the urban authority of Bhopal. As most of these villages do not have proper transport and communication facilities, not many people can commute to the city regularly to earn their bread. Except the very few persons who could manage to get jobs in BHEL as unskilled workers, the rest struggle for subsistence within the village. The villagers do not see much scope for animal husbandry and vegetable farming in the absence of adequate pasture or cultivable land. Again, the food which they grow in their fields is not sufficient for their sustenance and some grow vegetables in their fields mainly for consumption within the village. From the survey of these villages, it is clear that commercialisation of agriculture has not taken place. People in most of the villages still grow traditional food crops like wheat, paddy and jowar. Also, there are not many small agro-based industrial units even in the villages having more than 1,000 population. Under such circumstances, it is natural that the villagers would resent the location of the BHEL unit in Bhopal, as they consider it to be the reason for the loss of their economic occupation.

In some villages in the periphery, mechanization of agriculture seems to have taken place at a fast pace. But the ownership of land remains in the hands of a privileged few. Marginal farmers have been driven away from their lands because of the indebtedness and their extravagant spendings in marriage ceremonies, death rituals etc. This has led to more unequal distribution of lands and pauperisation of the marginal land-holders. In an attempt to confirm whether there has been a process of agricultural development or backwardness in Bhopal region, it was found from the agricultural statistics of M.P. that yield per hectare in Bhopal district is quite high in the case of both food crops and commercial crops, compared to the yield per hectare in M.P. in the year 1974-75. But the ratio of commercial crops to food grains is only 7.8 per cent in Bhopal district compared to the ratio of 13.46 per cent in M.P. in 1974-75. This shows the underdeveloped state of commercialisation of agriculture in the Bhopal region.

TABLE 7.1 : **Yield per hectare of food and cash crops, 1974-75.**

(*in quintals*)

Item	Yield per hectare during the year 1974-75	
	Madhya Pradesh	Bhopal
Food grains	6.05	7.95
Cash crops (sugarcane and oil seeds only)	4.30	7.80

Source : *Agricultural Statistics* 1974-75 Madhya Pradesh.

Table 7.1 above shows that although Bhopal is not agriculturally backward than the State as a whole, there is a scope for increasing the yield per hectare under foodgrains and cash crops on the lines of the developed districts of Punjab and Haryana. More area can be brought under cash crops like soyabean, groundnut, sunflower and other oilseeds, cotton, condiments and other spices. Similarly, various types of fruits like mango, pineapple, orange etc., and fresh vegetables can be grown in these villages for the increasing population of the city. Commercialisation of crops will increase the employment potential throughout the year and also help in the growth of agro-based industries in rural areas that can provide additional employment to its disguisedly unemployed and seasonally unemployed persons. Similarly, animal husbandry can be promoted in these areas by growing more animal feed. These activities coupled with a more balanced distribution of land (by implementing radical land reform measures) will definitely help in improving the lots of these deprived villagers. Even within the existing laws and social systems, the increasing commercialisation of agriculture and promotion of animal husbandry in these villages will solve the major problem of poverty. However, the other thing required for the success of the development efforts is the creation of social awareness among the people. This can be attempted by the government machinery through the adoption of demonstration programmes and launching of pilot projects.

At the time of the survey, most of the villagers complained that they gained nothing from the establishment of BHEL unit and most of the jobs in the unit went to the outsiders—to people from Punjab, U.P. and all Southern States—"although the local people sacrificed their land for the establishment of the unit". A total of 415 workers from the sample villages are employed in the BHEL unit as unskilled labourers and the number of workers employed by the unit goes down with the distance of the village from the Factory. In order to examine the validity of their statements, we undertook a separate survey to ascertain the state of origin of the workers in the oldest Block of BHEL factory, i.e Block IV which manufactures switchgear, control gear etc. Table 7.2 shows that the assertions of the villagers about the dominance of outsiders in all categories of jobs in the factory may not be totally correct. Starting from the post of executives to clerical staff and semi-skilled and unskilled workers, in Block-IV, the workers from M.P. are dominating the others. However, as most of the workers residing in Bhopal for a few years produce residential

TABLE 7.2 : **State-wise percentage distribution of workers in different industrial categories in Block-IV of BHEL unit in Bhopal, 1983**

S. No.	States	Executives	Supervisors	Artisans	Supporting technical staff	Semi-skilled and un-skilled	Clerical and others	Total
(1)	(2)	(3)	(4)	(5)	(6)	(7)	(8)	(9)
1.	Andhra Pradesh	5.80	1.04	1.61	—	0.45	—	1.47
2.	Arunachal Pradesh	—	—	0.11	—	—	—	0.07
3.	Assam	—	5.21	0.69	—	—	—	0.81
4.	Bihar	2.90	9.37	8.84	—	1.79	1.82	6.82
5.	Gujarat	—	—	0.23	—	—	—	0.15
6.	Haryara	1.45	2.08	1.03	—	—	—	0.88
7.	Himachal Pradesh	1.45	1.04	0.46	—	—	—	0.44
8.	Jammu and Kashmir	1.45	—	—	—	—	—	0.07
9.	Karnataka	2.90	1.04	0.57	—	—	—	0.59
10.	Karala	8.70	11.46	7.35	34.00	0.45	21.82	8.14
11.	Maharashtra	1.45	6.25	9.30	6.00	18.39	7.27	9.97
12.	Madhya Pradesh	23.19	10.42	44.89	36.00	41.26	54.55	40.84
13.	Meghalaya	—	—	—	—	—	—	—
14.	Mizoram	—	—	—	—	0.90	—	0.15
15.	Nagaland	—	—	—	—	—	—	—
16.	Orissa	—	—	0.23	—	—	—	0.15

TABLE 7.2 : (*Contd.*)

(1)	(2)	(3)	(4)	(5)	(6)	(7)	(8)	(9)
17.	Punjab	14.49	10.42	1.49	2.00	—	—	2.49
18.	Rajasthan	—	3.12	1.03	6.00	0.45	1.82	1.25
19.	Tamil Nadu	5.80	2.08	2.41	2.00	10.31	—	3.74
20.	Uttar Pradesh	15.94	11.46	14.24	14.00	24.66	12.73	15.76
21.	W. Bengal	2.90	8.33	4.71	—	—	—	3.74
22.	Sikkim	—	—	—	—	—	—	—
23.	Delhi	—	2.08	0.34	—	—	—	0.37
24.	Foreign countries	—	14.58	0.46	—	1.35	—	1.54
25.	Unspecified	11.59	—	—	—	—	—	0.59
	Total	100	100	100	100	100	100	100

Source : *Personnel Department*, BHEL, Bhopal, 1983.

certificate of M.P. Consequently, we took into account their states of origin and not their states of domicile. Thus, considering the advanced technology of production in the BHEL unit (Bhopal) which requires highly technical and skilled personnel, the percentage of jobs acquired by the people of M.P. is not very low, as indicated by the results of the survey in Block-IV.

Nevertheless, we cannot afford to ignore the damage done to the regional and rural economy of Bhopal due to the establish ment of BHEL factory and the increasing industrialization and urbanization of Bhopal City. There is no doubt that the benefit-cost ratio will be more than one if any project evaluation study is made by an expert on the BHEL unit in Bhopal. Also, we should not expect that each and every person in the working age group in the nearby villages will be provided with employment in the public sector unit which is established in a particular region. It is also obvious that a few acres of cultivable land from nearby villages will go waste in the process of acquiring land for a big key sector industry—for its factory and township. But the damage done to the rural economy can be repaired not by providing employment opportunities to the villagers in the factory itself, as it is impossible to provide jobs to each and every one within the unit. The policy formulators assume that when a big public sector industry is established in a particular region, it will automatically help the industrial growth of the region through forward and backward linkages and consequently the people displaced from agriculture will be absorbed in the industry. But actually this does not happen. The backwash effects, in general. outweigh the spread effects in a backward developing economy and thus do more damage to the regional economy. India is a country where the forces of modernity and traditions operate simultaneously. Especially, in the agricultural sector, people are guided more by traditions than by the operation of the market forces. Although the workers in the agricultural sector are paid money wages depending on their bargaining strength, in most of the cases the "paternal type" relationship prevails between the workers and the landowners. Workers feel more secure socially with that type of relationship than with, the contractual relationship prevailing in a market economy. This is why, although a worker in an industry earns more than the agricultural labourer in the Bhopal region, some of the agricultural workers prefer to work in villages than to go and work in the factories in Bhopal every day. Again the workers in small scale units feel more insecure because of whimsical operation of the private entrepreneurs. They do not have bargaining strength like their brethern working in large-scale public sector or private sector units. Whenever, they go on strike demanding more wages or other benefits, the industrialists take resort to lay-offs and lock-outs. Further, the earnings in terms of wages and other benefits of a BHEL worker, even in the unskilled category, are often higher than the earnings of a skilled worker in small-scale units in Bhopal. Thus, the people in rural areas of Bhopal as those in the city prefer to have a job in BHEL factory. Unfortunately, the rural people who are acquainted only with agricultural jobs find it difficult to get absorbed even as unskilled workers in the factory. When an agricultural worker moves to industry in the parallel type of jobs, he has to acquire some skills and for this he has to undergo a short period of apprenticeship. This, the worker in the nearby villages is not prepared to accept by sacrificing his present earning from agriculture which is the only source of his livelihood.

Under these conditions, the only option left for the development of these affected villages lies in the commercialisation of agriculture coupled with animal husbandry which will encourage the growth of agro and animal-based industrial units in the villages. Also, with the limited availability of land, more employment and more income can be generated for these rural households by changing the cropping pattern and by making agriculture more capital intensive. Again, the development of animal husbandry will solve the fuel problem in the villages and consequently the establishment of community based gobar gas plants can be an economically viable project. These plants will also help in the establishment of agro-based industries by supplying power to them. To develop these agriculture linked activities, the Government should take proper steps like dissemination of knowledge for the commercialisation of agriculture through its *lab to land* programme and by providing more subsidies in terms of seeds, pesticides, fertilizers etc. to the poor households and by purchasing their produce at reasonable prices. Besides, the Government should take proper steps for the security of workers in small scale units and provide them proper medical, education and transport facilities. Similarly, steps should be taken to reduce the high disparities in wages between big and small units. This is one of the main reasons that has discouraged the local workers in the city as well as in the countryside to leave agriculture or other traditional occupations and work in the small scale units.[2]

The study of the slums in Bhopal (Chapter 5) highlights the nature of job insecurity among the workers in small scale units and other urban based occupations. Although the wage rate is quite reasonable in Bhopal city, a worker fails to get work even for 20 days in a month. As a result more than 50 per cent of the households in slums live below the poverty line in highly distressed conditions. Efforts, therefore, should be made by the Government to improve their living conditions. The prevailing income disparity can result in serious social tensions among the workers belonging to different socio-economic strata. Because of the demonstration effects, a worker earning a subsistence living in a developed economy feels relatively more deprived than his counterpart in a backward economy. An industrial worker in Bhopal city would often evaluate himself in comparison to a BHEL worker. It is, therefore, important that the Government takes necessary steps through its programmes likes NREP, IRDP and Employment Guarantee Schemes (in the rural areas as well as in Bhopal city) to reduce income disparity within the city and slow down further immigration from the rural areas.

To sum up, we can say that the overall impact of a public sector unit like BHEL, Bhopal on its regional economy is positive, although the failure in adopting right strategies and policies to remove the 'back wash effects' of industrialisation and urbanisation has created some frustration among the population in the region. The solution to these problems can be sought in terms of :

(a) commercialisation of agriculture,
(b) diversification of the non-agricultural activities in the rural areas,
(c) creation of industrial job opportunities outside the Bhopal city but within the region, and
(d) ensuring job security and better wage and working conditions in the small scale units within the city and the region.

REFERENCES

1. See, *BHEL Ten Year Digest*, March 1981, p. 54.
2. The backwash effects of industrialisation, as discussed above, have been noted in case of several other big Public Sector enterprises as well. The study of the impact of the Rourkela Steel Plant on its regional economy conducted by the A.N. Sinha Institute of Social Studies, Patna has come up with similar conclusions.

APPENDIX—4.1

Description of the major groups of industries as per the National Industrial Classification

20—21 Manufacture of food products.

22 Manufacture of beverage, tobacco and tobacco products.

23 Manufacture of cotton textiles.

24 Manufacture of wool, silk and synthetic fibre textiles.

25 Manufacture of jute, hemp and mesta textiles.

26 Manufacture of textile products (including wearing apparel, other than foot wear).

27 Manufacture of wood and wood products, furniture, fixtures, etc.

28 Manufacture of leather, leather and fur products (except repairs).

29 Manufacture of paper and paper products, printing, publishing and allied industries.

30 Manufacture of rubber, plastic, petroleum and coal products.

31 Manufacture of chemical, and chemical products (except products of petroleum and coal).

32 Manufacture of non-metallic mineral products.

33 Basic metal and alloy industries.

34 Manufacture of metal products and parts except machinery and transport equipments.

35 Manufacture of machinery and machine tools and parts except electrical machinery.

36 Manufacture of electrical machinery, apparatus, etc.

37 Manufacture of transport equipment and parts.

38 Other manufacturing industries.

39 Repairs.

APPENDIX—4.2

Percentage of industrial units in broad groups to total units in Manufacturing and Repair Division, 1961 & 1971

Division 2-3 Major group*	M.P. % of units (R+U)		Sehore district % of units (R+U)		Bhopal city % of units	
	1961	1971	1961	1971	1961	1971
20—21	11.65	12.75	11.41	11.66	N.A.	16.67
22	17.71	12.28	1.85	2.08	,,	7.18
23	6.68	5.02	3.56	3.41	,,	1.62
24	0.53	0.78	0.07	0.01	,,	—
25	0.07	0.04	0.02	0.01	,,	—
26	7.03	10.67	11.72	15.75	,,	18.58
27	15.59	16.61	21.15	21.35	,,	7.75
28	0.15	0.27	0.68	0.74	,,	2.56
29	14.88	13.59	23.61	15.43	,,	3.77
30	0.04	0.11	0.15	0.31	,,	1.22
31	0.23	0.29	0.41	0.50	,,	0.85
32	8.14	9.62	8.44	8.01	,,	1.66
33	0.02	0.03	0.08	0.09	,,	0.24
34	9.69	8.83	8.25	6.58	,,	6.04
35	1.00	0.23	0.27	0.68	,,	1.54
36	0.07	0.02	0.47	0.14	,,	0.24
37	0.05	0.13	0.02	0.19	,,	0.49
38	5.41	4.72	4.33	3.77	,,	3.41
39	1.98	4.01	3.50	9.30	,,	26.17
Div. 2-3	100.00	100.00	100.00	100.00		100.00

* For codes see Appendix 4.1.

Source : 1. Census of India, 1961, *Housing and Establishment Tables*, Part IV-B, Vol. 8-Madhya Pradesh.

2. Census of India, 1971, *Establishment Tables*, Part III-B, Series 10-Madhya Pradesh.

Note : Data for the year 1961 have been adjusted according to the Guidelines of 1971 Census classification of major groups within the Manufacturing and Repair Division, to make these comparable with 1971 Census data.

APPENDIX—4.3

Percentage increase in the number of units in major groups within Manufacturing and Repair Division, 1961 and 1971

Division 2—3 Major group*		Percentage increase during 1961-71 (M.P.)	Percentage increase during 1961-71 (Sehore)
20—21	R	8.02	19.95
	U	14.95	13.64
	T	9.85	16.39
22	R	—34.70	—100.00
	U	—7.24	30.43
	T	—30.35	28.05
23	R	—30.13	9.23
	U	—2.63	9.14
	T	—24.42	9.18
24	R	28.33	—80.00
	U	50.46	—100.00
	T	47.04	—84.33
25	R	—46.88	—50.00
	U	—77.08	—
	T	—51.65	—50.00
26	R	53.76	57.02
	U	49.62	48.43
	T	52.50	53.08
27	R	4.86	5.79
	U	30.72	99.46
	T	7.08	15.02
28	R	166.67	—100.00
	U	80.03	33.93
	T	82.64	25.00
29	R	—8.79	—27.13
	U	—1.26	—10.15
	T	—8.28	—25.54
20—30	R	400.40	—
	U	181.63	138.46
	T	198.09	138.46
31	R	24.51	—
	U	33.10	50.00
	T	29.75	41.67

APPENDIX—4.3 (Contd.)

32	R	19.66	8.25
	U	8.72	7.14
	T	18.77	8.14
33	R	9.09	—
	U	37.68	28.57
	T	30.77	28.57
34	R	—9.51	—18.55
	U	0.40	19.23
	T	—8.52	—9.15
35	R	200.10	100.00
	U	122.98	179.17
	T	136.20	187.50
36	R	125.00	—
	U	—78.16	—66.67
	T	—75.42	—66.67
37	R	425.37	100.00
	U	50.38	550.00
	T	177.27	850.00
32	R	—15.52	—5.83
	U	—5.42	6.21
	T	—12.39	—0.78
39	R	65.44	225.81
	U	132.56	199.64
	T	103.52	202.25
Div. 2-3	R	—3.74	0.16
	U	21.11	46.32
	T	0.43	13.93

* For codes, see Appendix 4.1.
Source : Same as for Appendix 4.2

APPENDIX—4.4

Percentage of non-household industrial units and employment in major groups to all non-household units and employment in Manufacturing and Repair Division 1971

Division 2-3 Major group	MP's share in India		Sehore's share in M.P.		Bhopal's share in Sehore	
	% of units	% employed	% of units	% employed	% of units	% employed
1	2	3	4	5	6	7
20—21	4.71	3.50	3.92	4.98	64.01	46.79
22	3.94	6.69	4.68	2.11	72.73	69.00
23	2.35	5.10	2.88	2.20	53.85	89.03
24	0.89	3.93	0.00	0.00	0.00	0.00
25	0.90	0.33	0.00	0.00	0.00	0.00
26	5.26	4.20	6.17	5.36	69.62	72.59
27	4.40	4.93	5.48	4.21	66.80	62.52
28	2.86	2.99	8.09	7.02	86.30	92.54
29	4.45	2.98	4.92	5.99	76.92	76.54
30	2.76	1.48	8.36	3.60	96.77	97.26
31	2.78	1.99	4.64	6.83	54.84	73.85
32	2.80	2.39	1.98	0.39	45.00	35.09
33	2.34	7.22	10.23	7.45	66.67	32.83
34	3.24	2.96	5.44	13.13	70.59	19.47
35	1.97	3.22	8.93	6.91	61.02	7.82
36	0.98	3.05	21.54	70.47	42.86	1.55
37	1.95	2.33	5.76	0.46	90.91	90.62
38	3.47	2.36	2.85	2.37	70.00	74.19
39	4.94	5.02	8.27	7.16	77.68	86.99
Div. 2-3	4.11	3.86	5.35	5.57	70.60	44.95

Source : 1. Census of India, 1971, *Establishment Tables*, Part III-B (ii), Series I-India.

2. Census of India, 1971, *Establishment Tables*, Part III-B, Series 10-Madhya Pradesh.

APPENDIX—4.5

Percentage share of urban units in major groups to total units in Manufacturing and Repair Division, 1961 and 1971

Div. 2—3 Major group	Share of urban units in M.P.		Share of urban 1-9 person and unspecified person units in M.P.		Share of urban 10 & above person units in M.P.		Share of urban units in Sehore dist.	
	1961	1971	1961	1971	1961	1971	1961	1971
1	2	3	4	5	6	7	8	9
20—21	26.43	27.65	25.65	26.63	0.78	2.00	56.47	55.13
22	15.84	21.10	15.05	19.96	0.79	1.14	98.17	100.00
23	20.84	26.72	20.26	25.05	0.58	1.67	58.86	58.84
24	15.32	26.10	15.23	25.63	0.09	0.47	16.67	100.00
25	15.79	7.48	15.46	6.80	0.33	0.68	0.00	0.00
26	30.48	29.90	30.24	29.71	0.24	0.19	45.87	44.47
27	8.66	10.50	8.28	10.13	0.38	0.37	9.86	17.09
28	97.00	95.61	85.14	85.74	11.86	9.87	95.33	100.00
29	6.73	7.25	6.68	7.20	0.05	0.05	9.40	11.35
30	93.63	88.46	91.72	83.97	1.91	4.49	100.00	100.00
31	61.02	62.59	56.03	53.56	4.99	9.03	83.33	88.24
32	8.14	7.45	7.90	7.28	0.24	0.17	9.35	9.26
33	75.82	79.83	56.04	50.42	19.78	29.41	100.00	100.00
34	10.11	11.09	9.78	10.63	0.33	0.46	24.86	32.63
35	84.81	80.06	71.65	71.28	13.16	8.78	100.00	97.10
36	98.65	87.67	90.24	52.05	8.41	35.62	100.00	100.00
37	66.16	35.88	50.00	28.96	16.16	6.92	100.00	68.42
38	31.05	33.51	30.90	33.31	0.15	2.61	41.93	44.88
39	56.74	64.84	55.13	63.77	1.61	1.07	90.03	89.26
Div. 2—3	16.81	27.28	16.32	19.62	0.49	7.66	29.83	38.30

APPENDIX—4.5 (*Contd.*)

Major group	Share of urban 1-9 & unspecified person units in Sehore dist.		Share of urban 10 & above person units in Sehore dist.		Bhopal's share of units in Sehore dist.		Bhopal's share of 1-9 & unspecified person units in Sehore dist.		Bhopal's share of 10 & above person units in Sehore dist.	
	1961	1971	1961	1971	1961	1971	1961	1971	1961	1971
	10	11	12	13	14	15	16	17	18	19
20—21	55.18	53.94	1.24	1.19	N.A.	34.86	N.A.	33.93	N.A.	0.93
22	73.17	81.90	25.01	18.10	,,	84.29	,,	71.43	,,	12.86
23	55.06	56.81	3.80	2.03	,,	11.59	,,	11.01	,,	0.58
24	16.67	100.00	0.00	0.00	,,	0.00	,,	0.00	,,	0.00
25	0.00	0.00	0.00	0.00	,,	0.00	,,	0.00	,,	0.00
26	45.38	44.35	0.49	0.12	,,	28.77	,,	28.64	,,	0.09
27	9.43	16.81	0.43	0.28	,,	8.85	,,	8.61	,,	0.24
28	73.33	82.67	22.00	17.33	,,	84.00	,,	68.00	,,	16.00
29	9.40	11.15	0.00	0.20	,,	5.96	,,	5.77	,,	0.19
30	100.00	96.77	0.00	3.23	,,	96.77	,,	93.55	,,	3.22
31	83.33	80.39	0.00	7.85	,,	41.18	,,	37.25	,,	3.93
32	9.35	9.14	0.00	0.12	,,	5.06	,,	4.94	,,	0.12
33	100.00	66.67	0.00	33.33	,,	66.57	,,	55.55	,,	11.12
34	24.86	30.83	0.00	1.80	,,	22.41	,,	21.80	,,	0.61
35	100.00	86.96	0.00	10.14	,,	55.07	,,	55.07	,,	0.00
36	85.71	42.86	14.29	57.14	,,	42.86	,,	35.71	,,	7.15
37	50.00	68.42	50.00	0.00	,,	63.16	,,	63.16	,,	0.00
38	41.67	44.62	0.26	0.26	,,	22.05	,,	21.78	,,	0.27
39	89.07	87.77	0.77	1.49	,,	68.62	,,	67.13	,,	1.49
Div. 2—3	28.68	36.98	1.15	1.32	,,	24.38	,,	23.52	,,	0.86

APPENDIX—4.6

Major group-wise distribution of units and employment in Manufacturing and Repair Division, 1971

Div. 2-3 Major group	Madhya Pradesh Total (R+U)		Sehore Total (R+U)		Bhopal Total	
	% of units	% of employed	% of units	% of employed	% of units	% of employed
1	2	3	4	5	6	7
20—21	12.75	12.36	11.66	12.00	16.67	14.11
22	12.28	15.15	2.08	4.20	7.18	9.92
23	5.02	11.95	3.41	6.74	1.62	14.30
24	0.77	0.72	0.01	0.003	—	—
25	0.04	0.09	0.01	0.003	—	—
26	10.67	7.41	15.74	8.48	18.58	10.07
27	16.61	13.31	21.35	11.78	7.75	5.55
28	0.27	1.11	0.74	2.28	2.56	6.74
29	13.59	8.55	15.43	7.73	3.77	2.64
30	0.11	0.25	0.31	0.25	1.22	0.77
31	0.29	0.85	0.50	1.66	0.85	3.77
32	9.62	9.58	8.01	5.25	1.66	1.04
33	0.03	1.20	0.09	2.71	0.24	2.86
34	8.83	6.89	6.58	8.82	6.04	4.97
35	0.23	1.59	0.68	3.29	1.54	0.85
36	0.02	0.71	0.14	15.24	0.24	0.76
37	0.13	0.84	0.19	0.15	0.49	0.36
38	4.72	3.29	3.77	1.98	3.41	1.71
39	4.01	4.16	9.30	7.43	26.17	19.57
	100.00	100.00	100.00	100.00	100.00	100.00

Source : 1. Census of India, 1961, *Housing and Establishment Tables*, Part-IV-B, Vol. 8-M.P.

2. Census of India, 1971, *Establishment Tables.* Part III-B, Series 10-M.P.

APPENDIX—4.7

Types of industrial units in Bhopal and their production, 1983

Sl. No.	Type of units	Year of establishment			Total no. of units	State of origin		Type of ownership			No. of seasonal units	Ed. background of owners		No. of owners trained by BHEL	No. of regular skilled labourer
		Before 1961	1961-70	1971-83		Within the state	Outside the state	Proprietory, partnership	Pvt. Ltd. and Pub. Ltd.	Others		General	Technical		
1	2	3	4	5	6	7	8	9	10	11	12	13	14	15	16
1.	Engineering and machinery	—	6	13	19	9	10	18	—	—	—	4	15	1	455
2.	Electrical items	—	4	4	8	6	2	7	—	1	—	1	7	—	212
3.	Wood and wood products	—	1	3	4	2	2	3	—	1	—	1	3	1	56
4.	Chemicals	—	1	6	7	6	1	4	2	1	1	3	4	—	151
5.	Miscellaneous	2	1	9	12	7	5	10	1	2	3	7	5	—	673
6.	*Total*	2	13	35	50	30	20	42	3	5	4	16	34	2	1547

Source : Field Data, 1983.

APPENDIX 4.7 (*Contd.*)

Sl. no.	Type of units	No. of casual skilled labourer	No. of regular unskilled labourer	No. of casual unskilled labourer	Total number of workers	No. of units whose workers are trained in BHEL	No. of units whose workers are trained outside BHEL	No. of units getting raw materials locally	No. of units getting raw materials through agencies	No. of units getting raw materials from outside market	No. of units selling products to BHEL	No. of units selling products through the agencies	No. of units selling products to others
		17	18	19	20	21	22	23	24	25	26	27	28
1.	Engineering and machinery	12	320	35	822	1	1	6	18	7	15	3	10
2.	Electrical items	—	159	10	381	—	—	3	6	4	6	—	6
3.	Wood and wood products	—	31	15	102	1	1	1	3	1	3	1	2
4.	Chemicals	—	720	122	993	—	2	2	4	5	3	4	4
5.	Miscellanecus	—	1651	15	2339	—	1	5	5	5	4	3	7
6.	*Total*	12	2881	197	4637	2	5	17	36	22	31	11	29

APPENDIX—4.7 (*Contd.*)

Sl. No.	Type of units	No. of units buying inputs from BHEL	Fixed capital assets (Rs.)	Total value of input (Rs.)	Total value of output (Rs.)	Value of inputs supplied to BHEL (Rs.)	% of inputs supplied to BHEL to the total output
		29	30	31	32	33	34
1.	Engineering and machinery	5	2,53,68,393	1,80,85,044	3,98,00,699	1,96,67,000	49.41
2.	Electrical items	5	1,07,87,768	6,28,31,755	9,41,12,301	4,08,00,000	43.34
3.	Wood and wood products	—	23,03,544	56,72,919	89,15,108	80,95,281	90.80
4.	Chemicals	—	4,68,20,000	11,31,24,100	15,33,45,000	3,30,000	0.22
5.	Miscellaneous	—	2,11,78,089	5,45,94,480	9,33,07,492	18,80,000	2.01
6.	*Total*	10	11,24,57,694	24,53,08,298	38,94,80,600	7,07,72,281	18.17

Source : Field Data, 1983.

APPENDIX—5.1

Industrial classification of workers and non-workers by educational

State/ District	Total Population		Workers		Cultivators	
	1961	1971	1961	1971	1961	1971
1	2	3	4	5	6	7
(a) *Madhya Pradesh*						
1. Illiterate	56.48	50.44	15.94	10.03	2.04	0.97
2. Literate (without education)	27.82	19.13	10.56	5.30	0.68	0.41
3. Elementary	9.83	18.30	4.32	6.45	0.24	0.34
4 Matric	4.52	9.43	2.93	4.53	0.06	0.11
5. Tech. diploma	0.17	0.15	0.16	0.11	0.001	0.0007
6. Non-tech. dip.	0.006	0.01	0.0059	0.0058	0.0001	—
7. Univ. degree	0.97	2.12	0.75	1.42	0.01	0.02
8. Tech. degree	0.20	0.41	0.17	0.34	0.001	0.002
Total	100	100	34.94	28.09	3.04	1.87
(b) *Sehore dist.*						
1. Illiterate	58.30	48.62	16.96	9.08	0.78	0.39
2. Literate (Without education)	25.70	17.41	19.16	3.70	0.23	0.11
3. Elementary	6.47	16.90	2.52	5.96	0.06	0.13
4. Matric	6.55	12.43	4.41	6.47	0.04	0.07
5. Tech. diploma	0.99	0.61	0.97	0.53	0.001	0.001
6. Non-tech. dip.	0.008	0.04	0.007	0.02	—	—
7. Univ. degree	1.58	3.20	1.28	2.08	0.006	0.007
8. Tech. degree	0.41	0.79	0.37	0.62	—	0.002
(a) Eng. & tech.	0.17	0.28	0.167	0.24	—	0.001
(b) Medicine	0.063	0.19	0.59	0.16	—	—
(c) Agr. vet. & dairying	0.05	0.05	0.02	0.04	—	—
(d) Teaching	0.11	0.24	0.11	0.17	—	—
(e) Others	0.001	0.02	0.001	0.01	—	0.001
Total	100	100	36.67	28.47	1.11	0.72

levels in the urban areas of Sehore district in 1961 & 1971

Agricultural labourers		Mining/ forestry etc.		Household industry		Non-household industry		Construction	
1961	1971	1961	1971	1961	1971	1961	1971	1961	1971
8	9	10	11	12	13	14	15	16	17
0.73	1.34	1.12	0.71	2.21	0.96	2.26	1.57	1.57	1.08
0.06	0.16	0.33	0.20	1.02	0.52	2.46	1.21	0.49	0.19
0.01	0.09	0.10	0.17	0.20	0.40	0.83	1.42	0.15	0.17
0.004	0.01	0.10	0.14	0.02	0.08	0.44	0.83	0.18	0.08
—	0 0001	0.002	0.006	0.0002	0.0004	0.08	0.04	0.03	0.01
—	—	0.0001	0.0002	—	0.0001	0.0009	0.0006	0.0002	0.0004
0.0004	0.0004	0.02	0.03	0.001	0.004	0.08	0.14	0.02	0.01
—	—	0.007	0.007	0.0002	0.004	0.03	0.05	0.01	0.01
0.80	1.61	1.68	1.26	3.55	1.97	6.11	5.27	1.98	0.90
0.30	0.44	0.58	0.25	1.38	0.49	2.80	1.69	3.79	0.67
0.03	0.04	0.19	0.05	0.56	0.19	1.92	0.86	0.82	0.16
0.005	0.03	0.04	0.04	0.07	0.19	0.67	1.43	0.16	0.20
—	0.01	0.10	0.02	0.01	0.03	0.96	1.94	0.36	0.09
—	—	0.003	0.002	—	—	0.82	0.36	0.07	0.03
—	—	0.0004	—	—	—	0.0004	0.003	—	—
—	0.001	0.02	0.003	0.001	0.004	0.19	0.39	0.04	0.006
—	—	0.004	0.003	—	0.001	0.13	0.20	0.02	0.01
—	—	—	0.001	—	—	0.13	0.19	0.02	0.008
—	—	—	—	—	0.001	0.0004	—	—	—
—	—	0.003	0.002	—	—	—	0.005	—	—
—	—	—	—	—	—	—	0.002	0.0004	—
—	—	0.0007	—	—	—	—	0.002	—	0.001
0.33	0.52	0.94	0.36	2.01	0.91	6.90	5.27	5.27	1.17

APPENDIX—5.1 (*Contd.*)

State/District	Trade and commerce		Transport and communication		Other services	
	1961	1971	1961	1971	1961	1971
	18	19	20	21	22	23
(a) *Madhya Pradesh*						
1. Illiterate	1.45	1.04	0.86	0.77	4.15	2.24
2. Literate (without education)	2.38	1.08	0.85	0.46	2.29	1.07
3. Elementary	0.96	1.63	0.43	0.57	1.30	1.66
4. Matric	0.38	0.84	0.39	0.52	1.36	1.92
5. Tech. diploma	0.003	0.006	0.004	0.006	0.04	0.04
6. Non-tech. dip.	0.0003	0.0004	0.003	0.004	0.003	0.004
7. Univ. degree	0.07	0.30	0.05	0.07	0.50	0.85
8. Tech. degree	0.002	0.01	0.004	0.004	0.12	0.26
Total	5.28	4.76	2.58	2.40	9.84	8.05
(b) *Sehore dist.*						
1. Illiterate	1.75	1.13	1.05	0.84	4.53	3.18
2. Literate (without education)	2.38	0.83	0.86	0.31	2.80	1.16
3. Elementary	0.49	1.35	0.23	0.43	0.81	1.03
4. Matric	0.34	0.73	0.34	0.54	2.26	3.03
5. Tech. diploma	0.003	0.01	0.004	0.01	0.06	0.11
6. Non-tech. dip.	—	0.003	—	—	0.005	0.01
7. Univ. degree	0.08	0.35	0.06	0.10	0.88	1.22
8. Tech. degree	0.002	0.01	0.003	0.004	0.21	0.39
(a) Eng. & tech.	0.001	0.003	0.003	0.004	0.01	0.03
(b) Medicine	0.0007	—	—	—	0.06	0.17
(c) Agr. vet. & dairying	—	0.002	—	—	0.02	0.03
(d) Teaching	0.0004	0.002	0.0004	—	0.11	0.16
(e) Others	—	0.001	—	—	0.0003	0.008
Total	5.05	4.42	2.54	2.24	11.56	11.23

Source : 1. Census of India, 1961, *General Economic Tables*, Part II-B(i) Vol. 8-M.P.

2. Census of India, 1971, *General Economic Tables*, Part II-B(i) Series 10 M.P.

APPENDIX—5.2

Migrants to Bhopal city classified by educational levels and industrial categories 1961 and 1971

Migrant workers & non-workers	Total migrants		Illiterate		Literate (without edu. level)	
	1961	1971	1961	1971	1961	1971
1	2	3	4	5	6	7
Cultivators	0.23	0.23	56.77	37.21	25.94	12.79
Agricultural labourers	0.12	0.22	92.86	79.52	5.00	8.43
Other workers	47.98	38.06	41.59	23.54	27.13	10.48
Non-workers	51.68	61.49	54.26	41.63	29.50	18.54
Total	100	100	48.23	34.81	28.32	15.44

Sources : 1. Census of India, 1961, *Migration Tables*, Part II C (ii-A), Vol. 8, M.P.
2. Census of India, 1971, *Migration Tables*, Part II-D (Vol. 1), Series 10, M.P.

APPENDIX—5.2 (*Contd.*)

Elementary		Matric		Technical diploma		Non-tech. diploma		University degree		Technical degree	
1961	1971	1961	1971	1961	1971	1961	1971	1961	1971	1961	1971
8	9	10	11	12	13	14	15	16	17	18	19
7.52	25.58	6.01	17.44	—	1.16	—	—	3.76	3.49	—	2.33
1.43	7.23	0.71	4.82	—	—	—	—	—	—	—	—
7.31	20.17	15.75	30.20	1.70	2.90	0.009	0.06	5.31	9.62	1.03	3.02
8.66	20.27	6.44	15.48	0.04	0.22	0.005	0.02	1.06	3.34	0.03	0.50
8.00	20.11	10.98	21.07	0.84	1.24	0.007	0.03	3.10	5.73	0.51	1.46

APPENDIX—5.3

Select demographic characteristics in the slums surveyed in Bhopal

Sl. no.	Name of slum/ locality	Total no. of households	No. of households surveyed	Percentage of SC & ST households	Percentage of non-hindu households	Percentage of households above 5 members	Percentage of households below 5 members	Sex ratio	% of persons below 15 years	% of 15—60 yrs. persons	% of persons above 60 years	% of literates	% of Male literates	% of Female literates
1	2	3	4	5	6	7	8	9	10	11	12	13	14	15
1.	Arjun Nagar	176	7	57.14	42.86	71.43	28.57	600	37.50	60.00	2.50	62.50	72.00	46.67
2.	Subhas Nagar	186	7	42.86	0	28.57	71.43	1,000	43.33	56.67	—	33.33	46.67	20.00
3.	Bag Forhat Afja	89	5	0	100.00	60.00	40.00	937	46.16	48.39	6.45	54.84	68.75	40.00
3.	Sudhama Nagar	788	32	28.12	46.87	68.75	31.25	750	40.48	56.55	2.98	39.29	48.96	26.39
5.	Anna Nagar	1,000	40	62.50	15.00	52.50	47.50	895	45.00	50.00	5.00	38.33	52.63	22.35
6.	Lal Tanki	600	24	41.67	4.17	54.17	45.83	873	44.07	54.24	1.69	56.78	73.02	38.18
	Total	2,839	115	44.35	26.09	57.39	42.61	829	42.86	53.79	3.35	44.80	57.74	29.18

APPENDIX—5.3 (*Contd.*)

Sl. no.	Name of Slum/locality	% of graduate or tech. qualified persons	% of Schoolgoing children	% of Collegegoing persons	% of BHEL employees	% of daily labourers	% of indusirial workers excluding BHEL	% of persons in service	% of persons having a subsidiary occupation	% of self-employed households	% of earners	% of earners below 15 years
		16	17	18	19	20	21	22	23	24	25	26
1.	Arjun Nagar	5.00	25.00	0	5.00	31.25	35.50	31.25	6.25	0	42.50	13.33
2.	Subhas Nagar	0	16.67	0	0	55.56	33.33	11.11	0	0	30.00	0
3.	Bag Farhat Afja	3.23	22.58	3.23	0	27.27	27.27	45.45	0	0	35.48	7.14
4.	Sudhama Nagar	17.86	14.29	1.19	1.19	37.10	41.93	20.97	6.45	15.62	36.90	7.35
5.	Anna Nagar	1.67	12.22	0	2.22	36.51	39.68	23.81	4.76	22.50	35.00	1.23
6.	Lal Tanki	3.39	22.03	2.54	6.78	31.43	45.71	22.86	2.86	0	29.66	1.92
	Total	2.29	16.58	1.06	2.82	34.71	40.93	24·35	4.66	12.17	34.74	4.11

APPENDIX—5.3 (*Contd.*)

Sl. no.	Name of slum/locality	% of households having below Rs. 1,000 assets	% of households having Rs. 1,000-2,000 assets	% of households having above Rs. 2,000 assets	% of households having below Rs. 100 per capita monthly income	% of households having above Rs. 100 per capita monthly income	% of households from M.P.	% of households from outside M.P.	% of households living in the present locality for more than 5 years	% of household living in the present locality for less than 5 years	Previous occupation of the migrants before coming to Bhopal: % of agricultural or daily labourers	% of industrial workers	% of persons in service
		27	28	29	30	31	32	33	34	35	36	37	38
1.	Arjun Nagar	14.29	57.14	28.57	14.29	85.71	14.29	85.71	85.71	14.29	85.71	0	14.29
2.	Subhas Nagar	71.43	28.57	0	100.00	0	85.71	14.29	85.71	14.29	71.43	14.29	14.29
3.	Bag Farhat Afja	40.00	40.00	20.00	80.00	20.00	80.00	20.00	100.00	0	20.00	20.00	60.00
4.	Sudhama Nagar	62.50	25.00	12.50	56.25	43.75	46.87	53.13	90.62	9.38	56.25	12.50	31.25
5.	Anna Nagar	57.50	27.50	15.00	52.50	47.50	7.50	92.50	97.50	2.50	72.50	22.50	5.00
6.	Lal Tanki	50.00	45.83	4.17	45.83	54.17	30.00	70.00	95.83	4.17	70.83	4.17	25.00
	Total	54.78	33.04	12.17	53.91	46.09	32.17	67.83	93.91	6.09	66.09	13.91	20.00

Source : Slum Survey, 1983,

APPENDIX—5.3 (*Contd.*)

Sl. no.	Name of slum/locality	% of households preferring other than present occupation to raise their living standards seeking absorption in :					Amenities available in slum locality				
		BHEL	Agriculture and animal husbandry	Own workshop or business	Industry	Other services	Drinking water	Electricity	Distance from med. facility (kms)	Distance from market (kms.)	Distance from other services (kms.)
		39	40	41	42	43	44	45	46	47	48
1.	Arjun Nagar	28.57	42.86	42.86	0	0	Yes	No	6 to 10	1	1
2.	Subhas Nagar	0	0	14.29	0	0	Yes	Yes	2 to 4	1	0.5
3.	Bag Farhat Afja	0	0	60.00	0	0	Yes	Yes	0.5 to 05	1	1
4.	Sudhama Nagar	12.50	25.00	40.52	3.12	9.37	Yes	Yes	4 to 6	0.5	0.5
5.	Anna Nagar	7.50	5.00	57.50	0	2.50	Yes	Yes	1 to 6	2	2
6.	Lal Tanki	0	0	41.67	0	4.17	Yes	No	2 to 8	2	2
	Total	7.83	11.30	46.09	0.70	4.35	—	—	—	—	—

APPENDIX—5.4

Percentage distribution of population, workers and non-workers according to age groups in 1961 and 1971

Age group	Madhya Pradesh urban area					
	Population		Workers		Non-workers	
	1961	1971	1961	1971	1961	1971
1	2	3	4	5	6	7
0-14	39.53	41.99	2.52	2.02	60.0	57.61
15-59	55.87	52.99	92.12	91.84	35.56	37.81
60 & above+ANS	4.59	5.02	5.36	6.14	4.40	4.59
Total	100	100	100	100	100	100

APPENDIX—5.4 *(Contd.)*

Sehore district urban area						Bhopal urban agglomeration					
Population		Workers		Non-workers		Population		Workers		Non-workers	
1961	1971	1961	1971	1961	1971	1961	1971	1961	1971	1961	1971
8	9	10	11	12	13	14	15	16	17	18	19
38.47	42.16	2.60	1.89	59.24	58.18	37.77	41.80	2.45	1.83	58.44	57.86
57.09	50.50	92.84	92.83	36.40	33.66	58.04	50.55	93.59	93.40	37.24	33.34
4.43	7.34	4.56	5.28	4.36	8.16	4.18	7.64	3.96	4.77	4.32	8.80
100	100	100	100	100	100	100	100	100	100	100	100

N.B.—ANS=Age not stated.

Source : 1. Census of India, 1961, *General Economic Tab les*, Part II-B (i), Vol. 8-M.P.
2. Census of India, 1971, *General Economic Tables*, Part II-B (i), Series 10-M.P.

APPENDIX—6.1

Select demographic characteristics for India, Madhya Pradesh, Sehore and Bhopal districts, Huzur and Berasia tahsils and Bhopal city, 1961, 1971 and 1981.

Region	Population growth rate		Rural population growth rate		Urban population growth rate		% of urban population			% of rural S.C. population		% of urban S.C. population	
	1961-71	1971-81	1961-71	1971-81	1961-71	1971-81	1961	1971	1981	1961	1971	1961	1971
1	2	3	4	5	6	7	8	9	10	11	12	13	14
India	24.75	24.43	21.80	18.96	38.20	46.02	17.97	19.91	23.71	15.98	16.05	8.72	8.76
Madhya Pradesh	28.67	25.17	25.68	19.16	46.63	56.07	14.29	20.31	13.69	13.69	13.68	9.84	1.09
Sehore Dist.	37.13	28.59	31.65	25.35	65.28	54.63	36.01	43.40	13.31	20.89	21.72	6.27	6.46
Bhopal Dist.	53.93	55.56	25.96	18.44	71.32	73.79	61.66	78.72	76.26	21.99	22.55	5.35	5.86
Berasia Tahsil	25.74	29.72	25.83	28.92	24.75	39.36	7.73	7.67	8.24	21.27	23.49	13.69	11.83
Huzur Tahsil	61.74	62.35	26.10	7.01	72.62	74.69	66.61	81.76	87.78	20.82	21.84	5.12	5.74
Bhopal U.A.	107.61	74.69	—	—	107.61	74.69	—	—	—	—	—	5.58	5.74

APPENDIX—6.1 (*Contd.*)

Region	% of rural S.T. population		% of urban S.T. population		% rural literacy			% urban literacy			Rural sex ratio			Urban sex ratio		
	1961	1971	1961	1971	1961	1971	1981	1961	1971	1981	1961	1971	1981	1961	1971	1981
	15	16	17	18	19	20	21	22	23	24	25	26	27	28	29	30
India	8.15	8.37	0.98	1.19	19.C0	23.74	29.57	46.97	52.44	57.19	963	949	954	845	858	880
Madhya Pradesh	23.80	23.64	1.62	2.11	12.73	16.81	21.15	43.52	49.55	53.98	970	956	956	856	868	883
Sehore Dist.	6.04	7.44	0 43	0.60	10.09	14.33	19.47	41.70	51.37	47.78	911	900	914	787	829	871
Bhopal Dist.	1 95	2.61	0.44	0.60	9.20	13.66	16.89	43.07	53.22	56.38	890	877	888	773	823	866
Berasia Tahsil	—	2.13	1.07	1.05	8.29	11.97	—	24.21	35.88	—	892	874	—	841	880	—
Huzur Tahsil	2.00	3.13	0.42	0.59	10.20	15.51	—	43.59	53.57	—	887	880	—	771	822	—
Bhopal U.A.	—	—	0.44	0.59	—	—	—	43.16	53.57	56.72	—	—	—	807	822	866

APPENDIX—6.1 (*Contd.*)

Region	% of workers to total population (Rural male)			% of workers to total population (Urban male)			Primary sector males: % of cultivators to total workers (Rural)			Primary sector males: % of cultivators to total workers (Urban)		
	1961	1971	1981	1961	1971	1981	1971	1971	1981	1961	1971	1981
	31	32	33	34	35	36	37	38	39	40	41	42
India	58.17	53.46	52.21	52.40	48.82	48.18	61.09	55.99	55.26	5.56	5.21	5.26
Madhya Pradesh	61.58	55.28	55.21	52.44	46.70	46.70	67.36	65.22	64.47	6.89	6.65	7.25
Sehore Dist.	60.87	53.92	53.23	56.60	47.69	45.35	57.95	58.28	58.71	2.47	2.58	10.41
Bhopal Dist.	61.17	54.84	53.48	57.37	47.92	47.06	55.14	58.35	61.63	1.13	1.35	2.25
Berasia Tahsil.	61.65	55.11	—	52.73	44.15	—	59.15	61.70	—	7.33	11.32	—
Huzur Tahsil.	0.30	0.70	—	57.49	48.90	—	50.71	54.65	—	0.98	1.17	—
Bhopal U.A.	—	—	—	55.11	48.00	—	—	—	—	1.23	1.17	—

APPENDIX—6.1 (*Contd.*)

Region	Primary sector males											
	% of agr. lab. to total workers (Rural)			% of agr. lab. to total workers (Urban)			% of mining etc. workers to total workers (Rural)			% of mining etc. workers to total workers (Urban)		
	1961	1971	1981	1961	1971	1981	1961	1971	1981	1961	1971	1981
	43	44	45	46	47	48	49	50	51	52	53	54
India	15.75	25.21	24.26	2.21	4.66	4.74	3.25	2.95	—	2.47	2.64	—
Madhya Pradesh	15.90	21.95	20.70	1.38	3.93	4.38	3.72	2.46	—	4.70	4.53	—
Sehore Dist.	22.48	28.51	26.15	0.60	1.36	5.36	4.72	2.76	—	2.63	1.27	—
Bhopal Dist.	23.66	29.24	25.43	0.39	0.86	2.09	4.29	1.79	—	2.48	1.20	—
Berasia Tahsil	24.43	28.75	—	5.76	11.60	—	3.78	1.56	—	5.37	0.66	—
Huzur Tahsil	22.81	29.78	—	0.30	0.70	—	4.84	2.04	—	2.40	1.21	—
Bhopal U.A.	—	—	—	0.32	0.66	—	—	—	—	2.40	1.21	—

APPENDIX—6.1 (*Contd.*)

Region	Secondary sector males											
	% of household workers to total workers (Rural)			% of household workers to total workers (Urban)			% of non-household workers to total workers (Rural)			% of non-household workers to total workers (Urban)		
	1961	1971	1981	1961	1971	1981	1961	1971	1981	1961	1971	1981
	55	56	57	58	59	60	61	62	63	64	65	66
India	5.69	3.13	3.16	5.77	4.38	5.46	1.91	2.46	—	22.94	24.02	—
Madhya Pradesh	4.96	3.24	3.16	7.55	6.00	5.99	0.40	0.90	—	20.21	20.26	—
Sehore Dist.	5.28	3.97	3.38	4.03	2.90	7.02	0.60	0.80	—	23.20	25.54	—
Bhopal Dist	4.46	3.08	2.06	3.71	2.82	5.53	1.72	1.16	—	24.55	27.09	—
Berasia Tehsil	4.55	2.77	—	16.62	8.48	—	0.10	0.40	—	1.79	5.47	—
Huzur Tehsil	4.35	3.41	—	2.61	2.02	—	3.48	2.05	—	25.11	27.48	—
Bhopal U.A.	—	—	—	3.29	2.02	—	—	—	—	20.12	27.48	—

APPENDIX—6.1 (*Contd.*)

Region	Secondary sector males				Tertiary sector males			
	% of const. workers to total workers (Rural)		% of const. workers to total workers (Urban)		% of trade & com. workers to total workers (Rural)		% of trade & com. workers to total workers (Urban)	
	1961	1971	1961	1971	1961	1971	1961	1971
	67	68	69	70	71	72	73	74
India	0.89	0.82	3.85	3.57	2.62	2.77	18.00	21.42
Madhya Pradesh	0.70	0.50	5.97	3.33	1.47	1.54	17.05	18.29
Sehore Dist	0.70	0.60	13.10	13.81	1.68	1.66	15.30	16.50
Bhopal Dist.	0.92	0.72	14.63	3.99	1.67	1.43	14.67	15.83
Berasia Tahsil	0.20	0.20	3.58	3.72	1.35	1.30	19.19	25.11
Huzur Tahsil	1.66	1.27	14.90	3.99	2.02	1.57	14.56	15.66
Bhopal U.A.	—	—	12.06	3.99	—	—	15.33	15.66

APPENDIX—6.1 (*Contd.*)

Region	Tertiary sector males							
	% of transport and storage workers to total workers (Rural)		% of transport and storage workers to total workers (Urban)		% of other services workers to total workers (Rural)		% of other services workers to total workers (Urban)	
	1961	1971	1961	1971	1961	1971	1961	1971
	75	76	77	78	79	80	81	82
India	0.82	0.97	9.26	10.76	7.95	5.69	29.93	23.34
Madhya Pradesh	0.40	0.40	8.92	9.50	4.99	3.71	27.32	27.51
Sehore Dist.	0.50	0.40	7.90	8.43	7.08	4.10	30.77	37.61
Bhopal Dist.	0.94	0.45	8.55	8.90	7.20	3.79	30.66	38.65
Berasia Tahsil	0.02	0.09	4.76	5.80	6.34	3.25	35.59	27.84
Huzur Tahsil	1.95	0.80	8.64	8.95	8.16	4.39	30.53	38.85
Bhopal U.A.	—	—	9.82	8.95	—	—	35.00	38.85

Source : Census of India, 1961, 1971 and 1981, *General Economic Tables*, India and Madhya Pradesh ; Sehore, *District Census Handbook* for the years 1961 and 1971.

Note : The primary sector includes cultivation, mining, livestock, forestry etc. The secondary sector includes household industries, non-household industries and construction and the tertiary sector includes trade and commerce, transport, storage and communication and other services.

APPENDIX—6.2

Indicators depicting socio-economic conditions of the

Sl. no.	Name of village	Area in acres 1971	Growth rate of population	Sex ratio		% of SC population	
				1961	1971	1961	1971
1	2	3	4	5	6	7	8
1.	Lambakheda	1,335	31.56	894	907	18.44	18.05
2.	Palasi	552	27.87	1,021	921	21.60	0.27
3.	Badbai	1,862	45.86	835	839	15.83	22.69
4.	Islam Nagar	2,743	35.99	866	827	7.97	10.17
5.	Hatai Kheda	1,476	—65.40	891	865	38.31	38.34
6.	Khajuri Kalan	3,578	36.59	930	842	15.22	21.22
7.	Barkheda Pathani	1,833	44.26	896	918	35.94	26.07
8.	Pipaliya Penden Khan	404	43.45	867	875	10·12	19.17
9.	Bag Sewaniya	963	67.96	893	940	19.91	36.34
10.	Ahmadpur Kalan	420	—18.18	1,152	723	6.06	13.58
11.	Karhod Kalan	499	46.61	934	854	45.48	22.35
12.	Bhainsa Khedi	1,107	18.18	907	931	36.71	40.24
13.	Bhaonri	3,669	16.77	881	889	10.53	10.92
14.	Jamoniya Chhir	504	14.98	935	803	19.32	20.17
15.	Neelbad	698	36.02	1,175	952	38.86	37.98
16.	Mungaliya Chhap	3,266	16.18	847	890	18.37	15.46
17.	Bilkheda	1,372	—8.82	941	908	27.61	29.01
18.	Bishan Khedi	1,395	11.87	872	856	31.51	28.16
19.	Barkheda Nathu	1,427	29.53	880	897	22.48	26.04
20.	Gora	1,121	22.67	777	772	19.43	20.13
21.	Barkhedi Kalan	513	21.11	894	811	12.32	17.67
22.	Babadiya Kalan	2,562	32.86	921	901	14.72	14.51
23.	Bag Mungaliya	851	36.55	1,000	842	21.38	31.82
24.	Laharpur	412	32.43	1,176	1,162	13.51	17.69

selected villages around BHEL unit, 1961 and 1971

% of ST population		% of literates		% of male workers		Primary sector % of male cultivators		Sl. no.
1961	1971	1961	1971	1961	1971	1961	1971	
9	10	11	12	13	14	15	16	
0.84	—	20.67	23.57	50.26	55.87	34.74	31.88	1
—	—	23.34	30.52	57.04	53.40	33.33	26.47	2
0.18	9.00	13.49	19.48	61.06	53.97	31.35	29.41	3
—	0.69	12.78	17.59	51.64	50.87	40.25	44.27	4
—	14.74	15.31	18.50	60.88	49.00	10.09	17.35	5
—	—	6.16	12.64	54.78	54.56	68.51	58.51	6
—	0.35	10.48	19.15	59.94	52.65	39.47	27.73	7
—	—	17.26	16.25	52.22	50.00	44.68	39.06	8
—	—	7.79	9.28	62.29	56.50	50.00	37.17	9
—	—	18.18	18.52	65.22	48.94	26.67	21.74	10
0.56	—	5.65	29.86	61.20	48.93	52.68	39.42	11
—	—	7.34	19.82	60.67	53.71	34.07	31.91	12
1.52	1.07	14.72	25.06	57.38	52.52	56.14	51.10	13
—	—	11.11	21.01	57.94	46.21	46.77	45.90	14
—	6.62	12.80	16.03	58.76	57.14	56.14	42.86	15
0.32	—	11.06	12.04	58.86	50.53	48.50	52.88	16
—	—	7.66	18.57	59.91	38.83	48.12	67.50	17
—	—	7.31	6.12	62.39	59.85	43.84	51.90	18
—	—	10.23	13.73	65.61	54.05	70.67	61.82	19
—	—	0.81	1.98	52.52	59.06	64.38	66.34	20
—	—	7.92	2.42	64.44	56.14	84.48	66.41	21
1.42	4.00	18.04	23.73	51.50	56.52	28.78	27.16	22
—	—	9.31	17.93	57.93	52.09	22.62	44.64	23
3.60	—	6.31	16.33	70.59	61.76	44.44	57.14	24

APPENDIX—6 2 (*Contd.*)

Sl. no.	Primary sector males				Secondary sector males			
	% of agri. labourers		% of workers in mining etc.		% of workers in household ind.		% of workers in non-household ind.	
	1961	1971	1961	1971	1961	1971	1961	1971
	17	18	19	20	21	22	23	24
1.	41.05	33.33	1.05	5.07	3.16	2.17	—	—
2.	19.75	54.90	4.94	—	7.71	—	1.23	—
3.	39.46	36.13	11.35	13.44	4.32	3.78	1.62	7.56
4.	38.56	42.72	—	1.55	8.06	1.55	—	0.31
5.	4 61	29.59	17.00	7.14	7.49	8.16	15.27	2.04
6.	9.79	13.73	3.40	0.30	2.55	1.79	2.55	3.88
7.	10.00	46.38	5.26	2.10	6.32	3.36	9.47	26.47
8.	19.15	25.00	4.25	1.56	14.89	3.12	14.89	25.00
9.	17.10	16.81	6 58	2.65	3.95	0.88	9.21	13.27
10.	56.67	43.48	—	—	—	4.35	3.33	4.35
11.	29.46	32.12	2.68	2.92	3.57	2.92	0.89	0.73
12.	40.66	44.68	—	1.06	5.49	2.13	—	2.13
13.	20.47	21.15	3.51	1.65	8.77	7.97	0.58	1.10
14.	40.32	42.62	—	—	—	1.64	1.61	—
15.	14.03	28.57	3.51	3.57	5.26	4.76	—	—
16.	23.47	25.13	3.57	2.62	11.48	10.21	6.38	2.62
17.	32.33	28.75	12.78	—	0.75	—	—	—
18.	16.44	43.04	8.22	1.27	17.81	—	—	1.27
19.	12.98	27.27	1.44	—	2.88	—	—	4.54
20.	2.74	33.66	6.84	—	1.37	—	—	—
21.	0.86	30.47	—	—	1.72	—	—	—
22.	5.93	26.92	6.34	11.30	10.39	3.61	—	8.89
23.	73.81	29.46	—	0.89	1.19	1.79	—	15.18
24.	52.78	35.71	—	—	2.78	3.38	—	—

Tertiary sector males								
% of workers in construction		% of workers in trade and commerce		% of workers in transport and storage		% of workers in other services		Sl. no.
1961	1971	1961	1971	1961	1971	1961	1971	
25	26	27	28	29	30	31	32	
—	0.72	5.26	2.90	—	5.07	14.74	18.84	1
2.47	0.98	1.23	2.94	3.70	0.98	25.93	13.72	2
2.70	1.26	5.40	1.26	—	—	3.78	7.14	3
1.27	0.93	2.12	0.62	1.27	0.31	7.63	7.74	4
5.76	8.16	3.75	16.33	1.15	—	34.87	11.22	5
1.70	0.85	5.11	0.90	—	15.52	6.38	4.78	6
—	4.20	0.53	2.52	—	1.26	28.95	5.46	7
—	—	—	—	2.13	—	—	6.25	8
—	—	—	2.65	—	1.77	13.16	24.78	9
6.66	4.35	—	8.70	—	8.70	6.66	4.35	10
4.46	1.46	2.68	3.65	—	—	3.57	16.79	11
1.10	2.13	5.49	9.57	—	—	13.19	6.38	12
0.87	4.67	1.46	3.85	5.26	1.92	2.92	6.59	13
3.23	1.64	3.23	1.64	1.61	—	3.23	6.56	14
—	5.95	19.30	10.71	—	—	1.75	3.57	15
0.25	0.78	1.79	1.83	—	—	4.59	3.93	16
—	—	1.50	1.25	—	—	4.51	2.50	17
—	—	4.11	—	—	—	9.59	2.53	18
—	—	1.92	1.82	0.48	0.45	9.61	4.09	19
1.37	—	1.37	—	—	—	21.92	—	20
—	0.78	—	—	—	—	12.93	2.34	21
1.19	9.37	2.67	2.16	9.20	5.77	35.31	4.81	22
—	0.89	—	—	—	0.89	2.38	6.25	23
—	—	—	—	—	—	—	4.76	24

APPENDIX—6.3

Amenities available in selected villages

Sl. no.	Name of village	Total area (Acres)	% of irrigated land	% of unirrigated land	% of cultivable land
1	2	3	4	5	6
1.	Lamba Kheda	1,335	4.49	72.21	16.78
2.	Palasi	552	6.34	70.65	18.66
3.	Badbai	1,862	3.76	53.92	13.75
4.	Islam Nagar	2,743	16.26	55.49	12.14
5.	Hataikheda	1,476	2.78	15.65	55,28
6.	Khajuri Kalan	3,578	2.79	47.37	27.42
7.	Barkheda Pathani	1,833	0.49	33.93	20.02
8.	Pipaliya Penden Khan	404	1.24	27.23	20.54
9.	Bag Sewaniya	963	0.00	39.67	12.56
10.	Ahmadpur Kalan	420	1.67	62.14	14.05
11.	Karhod Kalan	499	0.40	88.18	1.00
12.	Bhainsa Khedi	1,107	1.63	28.00	4.34
13.	Bhaonri	3,669	0.38	62.11	16.65
14.	Jamoniya Chhir	604	2.98	59.77	11.42
15.	Neelbad	1,082	0.00	40.85	56.38
16.	Mungaliya Chhap	3,266	2.82	71.62	18.43
17.	Bilkheda	1,372	0.73	22.81	14.29
18.	Bishankhedi	1,395	0.21	29.89	6.52
19.	Barkheda Nathu	1,727	1.45	74.52	5.27
20.	Gora	1,121	0.36	60.48	2.14
21.	Barkhedi Kalan	513	0.00	72.32	11.89
22.	Babadiya Kalan	2,562	4.80	58.55	16.51
23.	Bag Mungaliya	851	0.59	67.10	1.06
24.	Laharpur	412	0.73	28.64	0.97

around BHEL unit, 1971

% of area not available for cultivation	Distance from Bhopal city (Kms.)	Communication	Education	Medical	Power supply	Drinking water	Sl. no.
7	8	9	10	11	12	13	
6.52	8	PR	MS	—	E,EI,EIN	W	1
4.35	5	PR	PS	—	E	W	2
28.57	8	KR	PS	—	E	W	3
16.11	10	PR	PS, MS	—	E,EI,EIN	W	4
26.29	17	PR	MS	FC	—	T,W	5
22.41	12	KR	PS	—	E,EI,EIN	W	6
45.55	14	PR	MS	—	—	W	7
50.99	14	PR	PS	—	—	W	8
47.47	11	PR	PS	—	—	W	9
22.14	10	PR	—	—	E,EI,EIN	W	10
10.42	3	PR	PS	—	—	W	11
66.03	10	PR	PS	—	E,EI,EIN	W	12
20.85	14	PR	MS	—	EI	W	13
25.83	16	PR	MS	—	EI	W	14
2.77	17	KR	—	—	—	W	15
7.13	19	KR	MS	—	—	W	16
62.17	9	KR	PS	—	—	W	17
53.37	9	KR	—	—	—	W	18
18.76	11	KR	PS	—	—	W	19
37.02	6	KR	PS	—	—	W	20
15.79	8	PR	PS	—	—	W	21
20.14	14	PR	PS	—	E,EI,EIN	W	22
31.36	14	KR	—	—	—	W	23
69.66	15	KR	—	—	—	W	24

PR=Pucca Road
KR=Kutcha Road
PS=Primary School
MS=Middle School
E=Electricity
EI=Electricity for irrigation
EIN=Electricity for industries
W=Well water
T=Tap water
FC=Family Planning Centre

Source : Census of India, 1971, *District Census Handbook*, Sehore.

APPENDIX—6.4

Indicators constructed through the survey of the select villages

Sl. no.	Name of village	Population	% of SC & ST pop.	% of cultivator per household	% of daily lab & agr. lab per household	BHEL worker per 100 household	BHEL worker per 100 pop.	% of milk producing household
1	2	3	4	5	6	7	8	9
1.	Lambakheda	900	33.33	25.00	50.00	5.00	1.11	7.50
2.	Palasi	450	11.11	42.86	35.71	2.86	0.44	7.14
3.	Badbai	480	25.00	20.00	80.00	1.00	0.21	15.00
4.	Islam Nagar	2,000	5.00	25.00	62.50	0.50	0.10	3.00
5.	Hatai Kheda	700	85.71	10.00	78.57	11.43	1.14	5.71
6.	Khajuri Kalan	3,000	13.33	58.33	16.67	33.33	6.67	25.00
7.	Barkheda Pathani	2,500	16.80	25.00	72.50	6.67	1.60	6.67
8.	Pipaliya Penden Khan	400	50.00	7.14	64.29	14.29	2.50	11.43
9.	Bag Sewaniya	500	10.00	27.78	5.56	55.56	10.57	5.56
10.	Ahmadpur Kalan	200	6.00	80.00	20.00	20.00	1.00	30.00
11.	Karhod Kalan	1,500	8.33	35.56	20.00	—	—	42.22
12.	Bhainsa Khedi	450	38.89	33.33	26.67	8.00	1.33	53.33
13.	Bhaonri	2,500	14.00	40.00	50.00	—	—	2.00
14.	Jamoniya Chhir	300	50.00	20.00	50.00	10.00	2.00	16.67
15.	Neelbad	400	50 00	35.71	50.00	—	—	20.00
16.	Mungaliya Chhap	3,000	16.67	33.33	63.33	0.17	0.03	1.67
17.	Bilkheda	315	19.05	16.00	66.67	1.33	0.32	4.00
18.	Bishan Khedi	300	20.00	26.67	73.33	—	—	3.33
19.	Barkheda Nathu	1,000	33.33	90.00	10.00	—	—	8.00
20.	Gora	250	24.00	66.67	33.33	—	—	20.00
21.	Barkhedi Kalan	1,000	25.00	20.00	80.00	—	—	4.80
22.	Babadiya Kalan	2,900	20.69	25.00	66.67	8.50	1.72	2.50
23.	Bag Mungaliya	600	33.33	50.00	10.00	15.00	2.50	25.00
24.	Laharpur	325	30.77	44.44	26.67	13.33	1.85	15.55

around BHEL unit, 1983

% of households having livestock	% of households growing vegetable	% of households selling wood	% of households doing stone work	% of households in construction	% of household in household industry	% of households in NH industry excluding BHEL	% of households in trade & commerce	% households in service	Sl. no.
10	11	12	13	14	15	16	17	18	
2.50	5.00	1.50	—	—	2.50	10.00	1.00	30.00	1
—	—	—	—	—	2.86	—	—	7.14	2
—	10.00	—	—	—	3.00	—	—	—	3
1.00	6.25	—	—	—	1.75	—	0.75	6.75	4
—	2.86	—	—	—	2.86	—	—	—	5
—	4.17	—	—	13.33	1.00	2.50	0.33	0.66	6
—	1.67	—	—	5.83	1.33	—	0.83	—	7
—	—	—	—	—	—	—	—	2.86	8
—	—	3.33	—	—	—	—	—	11.11	9
—	20.00	—	—	—	—	—	—	—	10
—	2.67	—	—	—	2.22	—	0.89	13.33	11
—	6.67	—	—	—	—	—	2.67	26.67	12
—	3.00	—	—	—	—	—	0.80	3.20	13
—	5.00	—	—	—	—	—	—	—	14
—	4.29	—	21.43	—	4.29	—	—	—	15
2.00	—	—	—	0.83	—	0.83	0.50	1.00	16
1.33	—	—	—	—	—	—	—	12.00	17
—	10.00	—	—	—	—	—	—	—	18
2.00	12.00	—	—	—	2.00	—	—	2.80	19
—	—	—	—	—	—	—	—	—	20
—	2.40	—	—	—	—	—	—	—	21
—	2.50	—	—	—	0.17	—	1.00	3.33	22
—	—	—	2.00	—	—	—	—	4.00	23
4.45	—	2.22	—	—	—	—	—	—	24

APPENDIX—6.5

Amenities available in selected villages around BHEL unit in 1983

Sl. no.	Name of village	Distance from the city (km)	Distance from the BHEL unit (km)	Edu. facilities	Distance of primary school (km)	Distance of middle or High School (km)	Distance of college (km)	Distance of med. institute (km)	Drinking water	Electricty	Fuel	Communication
1	2	3	4	5	6	7	8	9	10	11	12	13
1.	Lambakheda	8	18	MS	0	8	8	8	No	Yes	No	PR
2.	Palasi	5	16	PS	0	7	7	8	No	Yes	No	KR
3.	Badbai	8	18	PS	0	8	9	8	No	Yes	No	KR
4.	Islam Nagar	10	20	MS	0	10	10	0(PC)	Yes	Yes	Yes	PR
5.	Hatai Kheda	17	6	PS	0	7	15	3	Yes	Yes	No	KR
6.	Khajuri Kalan	12	5	PS	0	5	10	5	No	Yes	No	KR
7.	Barkheda Pathani	14	3	MS	0	3	7	14	Yes	Yes	No	PR
8.	Pipaliya Penden Khan	14	3	PS	0	3	10	8	No	No	No	PR
9.	Bag Sewaniya	11	3	PS	0	3	10	5	No	No	Yes	PR
10.	Ahmadpur Kalan	10	6	Nil	1.5	10	11	11	No	Yes	No	PR
11.	Karhod Kalan	4	12	MS	0	4	4	0(PC)	Yes	Yes	Yes	PR
12.	Bhainsa Khedi	10	19	PS	0	2	2	2	Yes	Yes	No	PR
13.	Bhaonri	15	24	MS	0	5	5	5	Yes	Yes	No	PR
14.	Jamoniya Chhir	14	23	PS	0	6	7	6	Yes	Yes	No	PR

APPENDIX—6.5 (*Contd.*)

15.	Neelbad	12	18	PS	0	3	12	12	No	Yes	No	KR
16.	Mungaliya Chhap	16	25	HS	0	0	18	0	Yes	Yes	No	KR
17.	Bilkheda	9	22	PS	0	2	16	8	Yes	Yes	No	KR
18.	Bishan Khedi	9	22	PS	0	4	10	4	No	No	No	KR
19.	Barkheda Nathu	11	25	SS	0	0	11	3	Yes	Yes	No	KR
20.	Gora	6	16	PS	0	7	7	7	No	No	No	KR
21.	Barkhedi Kalan	8	17	PS	0	4	8	6	No	Yes	No	PR
22.	Babadiya Kalan	14	8	MS	0	14	14	14	Yes	Yes	Yes	PR
23.	Bag Mungalia	14	4	PS	0	9	9	9	Yes	Yes	No	KR
24.	Laharpur	15	6	No	2	3	10	3	No	Yes	No	KR

Source : Village Survey, 1983.

Note : HS—High School PC—Private Clinic

For other abbreviations used, see Appendix 6.3

BIBLIOGRAPHY

Books

Brown, L. Dane *et al.*, *Public Enterprises as Catalysts of Rural Development* (New Delhi : PECCE, 1980).

Das, S., *Our Public Sector Undertakings : A Critical Estimate* (Calcutta : Delight Book, 1968).

De, Nitish R., *Perspective on Public Enterprises* (Delhi : Manchester Book Service, 1978).

Fernades, P.J., *Public Enterprises in India—A Perspective View* (New Delhi : SCOPE, 1974).

Fitzerland, E.V.K., *Public Sector Investment Planning for Developing Countries* (Delhi : MacMilan, 1979).

Ganguly, D.S., *Public Corporations in National Economy with Special Reference to India* (Calcutta : Book Land, 1963).

Gupta, K.R., *Issues in Public Enterprises* (Delhi, 1969).

Hoover, E.M., *The Location of Economic Activities* (New York, 1948).

Khera, S.S., *Establishment of the Heavy Electrical Plant at Bhopal* (New Delhi : IIPA, 1963).

Kolesov, V., *The Public Sector : An Effective Means of Development* (New Delhi : Sterling, 1980).

Mishra, G.P. (ed.), *Regional Structure of Development and Growth in India*, Vol. I (New Delhi : Ashish, 1985).

Mishra. G.P. and Joshi, A., (eds.), *Regional Structure of Growth and Development in India*, Vol. II (New Delhi : Ashish, 1985).

Mohammed Mohsin, *Chittaranjan--A Study in Urban Sociology* (Bombay : Popular Prakashan, 1964).

Moore, Wilbert E., *The Impact of Industry* (New Delhi : Prentice Hall, 1969).

Nigam, Raj K. (ed.), *National Aspiration and Public Sector* (New Delhi, SCOPE, 1976).

Patel, M.L., *Dilemma af Balanced Regional Development in India* (Bhopal : Progress Publishers, 1975).

Pillai, S. Devdas and Baks, Chris (eds.), *Winners and Losers :*

Style of Development and Change in an Indian Region (Bombay : Popular Prakashan, 1979).

Prem, Pardeep, *et al.*, *A Review of the Role of Public Enterprises in Indian Development* (New Delhi : PECCE, 1980).

Ramaswamy, T., *Public Enterprises in India : Objectives and Performance* (Delhi : Meenakshi Prakashan, 1972).

Shirokov, G K., *Industrialisation of India* (New Delhi : People's Publishing House, 1980).

U.N.E.S.C.O., *Social Implications of Industrialisation and Urbanisation* (Calcutta : UNESCO Research Centre, 1956).

Government and Special Publications

Annual Reports : Heavy Electricals (India) Limited, 1956-57, 1957-58, 1958-59, 1959-60, 1960-61, 1961-62, 1962-63, 1963-64, 1964-65, 1965-66, 1966-67, 1967-68, 1968-69, 1969-70, 1970-71, 1971-72, 1972-73.

Annual Reports : Bharat Heavy Electricals Limited, 1973-74, 1974-75, 1975-76, 1976-77, 1977-78, 1978-79, 1979-80, 1980-81, 1981-82 (New Delhi : BHEL).

BHEL, *Township—A City within a City* (Bhopal : BHEL, 1977)

BHEL, *Ten Year Digest* (New Delhi : BHEL, 1981).

BHEL, *Facts at a Glance* (Bhopal : BHEL, 1981, 1982).

DIC, Four Years Action Plan 1979-83 (Bhopal : District Industry Centre, 1979).

Government of India, *Build Machines Build India* (New Delhi : Director of Public Relations, 1969).

Administrative Reforms Commission, *Report of the Study Team on Public Sector Undertakings*, (Delhi : Manager of Publications, 1967).

Committee on Public Undertakings, (COPU), *Fifth Report*, *Action taken by Government on the Recommendations contained in the Twelfth Report of the Committee on Public Undertakings on Heavy Electricals (India) Limited*, (New Delhi : Lok Sabha, 1971).

Committee on Public Undertakings (COPU), *Fourtieth Report on Role and Achievements of Public Undertakings* (New Delhi : Lok Sabha ; 1975).

Committee on Public Undertakings (COPU), *Seventy-Second Report*, *Action taken by Government on the Recommendations Contained in the Fourtieth Report of the Committee on Public*

Undertakings (New Delhi : Lok Sabha, 1975).

Lok Sabha, *Role and Achievements of Public Undertakings* (New Delhi : 1973).

Ministry of Finance, Bureau of Public Enterprises, *Annual Reports, on the Working of Industrial and Commercial Undertakings of the Central Government*, 1973-74, 1974-75, 1975-76, 1976-77, 1977-78 and 1978-79. Vol. I, II and III (Delhi : Manager of Publications).

Ministry of Finance, Bureau of Public Enterprises, *Public Enterprises Survey*, 1979-80, 1980-81, 1981-82, Vol. I, II and III (Delhi : Manager of Publications).

T.C.P.O., *Bhopal Development Plan* (Bhopal : Alok Press, 1973).

Articles

Asthana, P., "Institutional Finance for Industry and Regional Disparities in India", in G.P. Mishra (ed.), *Regional Structure of Development and Growth in India*, Vol. I, (New Delhi : Ashish, 1975).

BALCO, *Lok Udyog*, December, 1979.

Chander, Bal., "Public Opinion and Public Sector", *Lok Udyog*, November, 1972, pp. 35-39.

Gupta, S., "The Role of Public Sector in Reducing Regional Income Disparity in Indian Plan", *Journal of Development Studies*, *9* (*2*), January, 1973, pp. 243-260.

Hansen, A.H,, "Public Enterprises and Economic Development", *AICC Economic Review*, September, 1969.

Jussawalla, M.F., "Efficiency and the Public Sector", Lok Udyog, 5 (3), June, 1971, pp. 271-274.

Kashyap, S.P., "Government Sponsored Industrial Growth : The Jaipur Industrial Estate—A Case Study", *Economic Weekly*, 16 (25), June 20, 1964, pp. 1021-1028.

Khan, A.F., "Social Responsibilities of Public Enterprises", *Lok Udyog*, August, 1971.

Malegam, Y.H., "Performance Evaluation of Public Enterprises", *Lok Udyog*, 4 (3), 1970, pp. 417-424.

Mani, M. and Das, A.N., "Public Enterprises in Rural Development—A Survey", *Towards Continuing Education*, December, 1979.

Mani, M. and Das, A.N., "Report on the Activities of Public Enterprises in the Field of Rural Development", *Towards*

Continuing Education, December, 1980.

Mukherjee, Ramakrishna, "Sociologists and Social Change in India Today", *Sociological Bulletin*, Vol. 11, March-Septembr, 1962.

Nair, M.V., *et al.*, "Need for New Policy Perspectives on Regional Development", *Lok Udyog*, August 1976, pp. 17-27.

Nanjappa, K.L., "Ancillary Development, Need for Subcontracting Exchanges", *Lok Udyog*, 4 (9), July 1970, pp. 1051-56.

Nath, Ashok, "Regional Development and Public Sector—A Case Study of North-Eastern Region", *Lok Udyog*, December, 1976.

Nath, V., "Regional Development in Indian Planning", *Economic and Political Weekly*, Annual Number, January, 1970.

Nayar, M.K.K., "Ancillary Industries—The Inescapable Responsibilities of the Public Sector", *Lok Udyog*, January, 1973, pp. 17-20.

Nigam, R.K., "Role of Public Sector in Socio-Economic Transformation", *Lok Udyog*, 10 (1), April, 1976.

Pathak, H.N., "Small Scale Industries in Ludhiana", *Economic and Political Weekly*, 5 (28), July, 1970, pp. 1091-97.

Puri, Y.P., "Of Eyes and Ears in Public Undertakings", *Lok Udyog*, June, 1972, pp. 5-12 and July, 1972, pp. 15-28.

Ranga, S., "Social Good Determines Public Sector Image", *Public Undertakings*, November, 1973.

Ranganathan, V., "The Public Sector and the Social Cost-Benefit Analysis", *Lok Udyog*, 10 (5), August 1976, pp. 41-48.

Rao, P. Prabhakar and Sundaram, K.V., "Regional Imbalances in India : Some Policy Issues and Problems", *Indian Journal of Regional Science*, 5 (1), 1973, pp. 61-80.

Ray, Sankar, "Public Sector and Socio-Economic Change" *Mainstream*, 18 (34), April, 1980, pp. 19-21.

Sanjivaya, D., "Public Sector—An Investment of Social Transformation", *Public Undertakings*, August, 1970.

Satyamurthi, Y., "Image of Public Sector", *Lok Udyog*, 6 (2), May, 1972, pp. 17-22.

Satyanarayana, *et al.*, "Socio-Economic Impact of a Public Sector Unit—A Case Study of Mining Projects in the Backward Regions of Orissa and Madhya Pradesh", *Lok Udyog*, June, 1973, pp. 5-14.

Shah, Mridula M., "Commercial Profitability *Vs.* Social Profitability", *Lok Udyog*, 1 (7), September, 1967, pp. 17-22.

Sinha, T.N., "Social Obligations of Public Undertakings", *National Investment and Finance*, 14th August, 1977, pp. 22-81.

Sondhi, M., "Steel and Heavy Industry in Rural Development", *Human Futures*, Spring, 1978, pp. 35-40.

Thimmaih, G., "Inter-State Disparities in Financial Allocations by the Centre", in G.P. Mishra and A. Joshi (eds.) *Regional Structure of Development and Growth in India*, Vol. II, (New Delhi : Ashish, 1985).

Venu, S., "Profitability and Social Responsibility", *Lok Udyog*, November, 1971, pp. 775-76.

Wadhawan, M.P., "Public Sector Steel Industry in India—Evaluation of Financial and Physical Performance" *Lok Udyog*, November, 1979, pp. 21-29.

Theses and Project Reports

A.N. Sinha Institute of Social Studies, *Regional Distribution of Economic Benefits arising from a Steel Plant—A Case Study of Rourkela Steel Plant* (Ranchi : Statistics Division, H.S.L., 1975).

Naidu, W.G., *A Study in Depth of some Aspects of Management of HE (I) L* (Ph.D. Thesis), (Nagpur University, 1980).

Ramaswamy, N.S. and Shivaramu, S., *Summary of the Micro Studies--Performance of Public Enterprises in Asia Project*, (*Sponsored by IDRC*) (Mimeographed) (Bangalore : IIM, 1977).

Shivaramu, S., *A System Study on BHEL—Draft Report* (Sponsored by IDRC), (Mimeographed) (Bangalore : IIM, 1977).

Press Clippings

Banerji, A.N., "Public Sector Projects and Social Objectives", *Economic Times*, 22nd November, 1971, p. 4.

Bhatt, Tushar, "Public Sector Project's Impact on People of Backward Areas, *Economic Times*, 8th October, 1972, p. 4.

Kakkar, Mulk Raj, "Dispersal of Industries and Backward Areas", *Economic Times*, 3rd and 4th September, 1967.

"Editor, Public Sector to go to Backward Areas", *Economic Times*, 3rd July, 1980, pp. 2-5.

Editor, Stress on Social Obligations of Public Sector, *Financial Express*, 26th August, 1979, 1, 2-7.

INDEX